The World's FASTEST CARS

AN ILLUSTRATED GUIDE TO HIGH PERFORMANCE PRODUCTION CARS

COMPLETELY REVISED

THE WORLD'S FASTEST CARS

GILES CHAPMAN & JOHN McGOVREN

A QUINTET BOOK

Published by Chartwell Books
A Division of Book Sales, Inc.
110 Enterprise Avenue
Secaucus, New Jersey 07094

ISBN 1-55521-670-6

This book was designed and produced by
Quintet Publishing Limited
6 Blundell Street
London N7 9BH

Creative Director: Peter Bridgewater

Typeset in Great Britain by
Central Southern Typesetters, Eastbourne
Manufactured in Hong Kong by
Regent Publishing Services Limited
Printed in Hong Kong by
Kwong Fat Offset Printing Co., Ltd.

Contents

INTROD

It is not easy to decide which single country, if any, is the true home of the fast car, as so many countries can put forward a claim, of sorts. On any enthusiast's short list of really fast cars, however, half a dozen makes will inevitably dominate the top places: Ferrari, Porsche, Lamborghini, BMW, Maserati and Mercedes-Benz. Why this should be is probably obvious, even to the layman, but there are other considerations affecting my choice that need some explanation.

Let's start with Italy, a marvellous country of passionate people with an intense love of competition, not only in things sporting but in life in general. They have a long standing addiction to speed, be it of the pedal-driven two-wheel variety, or the powered kind. Italy was the first country in the world to develop a system of high speed inter-city motor roads and that served to filter out the lame, halt and unfit automobiles of the time, leaving only tough and reliable machines to go on to greater things. In the great days of automobile competition Italy was a country that seemed to support more races than there were days on the calendar. The sport of auto-racing, however, could not have developed in Italy without the fullest support of the government, people, and industry. These factors have made sure that, in spite of any other problems, Italians continue to love the fast car.

In recent years Italy has been burdened with a national system of speed limits; at the time of their introduction it was feared that they might prove to be the beginning of a cooling-off of the Italian love affair with speed but after several years there is little evidence of any reduction in this love. The Italians still make fast cars and they still drive fast cars fast!

Neither the Italians nor the Germans believe in the nonsense that speed kills; both appreciate that it is the unskilled driver who does all the damage. They know that if the driver is educated properly, given good equipment to use and good roads on which to use it the end result is not only greater respect for speed but also a deal more fun in using it safely. Italian fast cars have always been among the quickest anywhere for their day and the Italian racing colour of red is still the only *really* appropriate colour for an Italian car — be it a Fiat Topolino or a Ferrari Daytona coupé!

Italians love the automobile with a fervour that only a Latin race could display and their excitement can be recognized as a result of the Italian car itself. Having owned Italian cars as diverse as a 1938 Lancia Aprilia, a 1971 Lancia Fulvia and a 1972 Fiat 130 saloon, I can attest to the fact that each displayed a verve, a *brio* (to use a very appropriate Italian word) that few other cars of the time, if any, could approach. They all cried out to be driven as fast as the road and conditions allowed, yet all retained the secure and sure-footed feel of a real thoroughbred. Such a feeling comes only from an integrity on the part of a car maker who realizes that his products will be used hard — and so makes sure that his cars will not be found wanting.

The automobile designer and engineer in Italy hold a very special place in that country's social strata. They are highly respected — or, in the case of Enzo Ferrari, virtually worshipped — by the ordinary people. This factor alone must have a tremendous bearing on the quality of the Italian fast car. Technical education and the competitive nature of Italian industry throw up great engineers, designers, innovators and managers with great speed. The same background has also created some of the world's greatest competition drivers. To car enthusiasts the world over, names like Pininfarina, Nuvolari, Ascari, Bertone, Giugiaro, Jano, Lamborghini and Agnelli are part of the very fabric of motoring.

Italy not only provided support and enthusiasm for the automobile and its use but also offered one of the most perfect proving grounds for the refinement of the car. Until recently virtually all Italian car production was concentrated in the north, in and around the cities of Turin and Milan. To the north of these lie the mountains, to the west and the south west are the plains. The former test the agility, acceleration, roadholding, steering and braking of any car, while the fast straight roads of the latter, stretching for mile after mile, expose any shortcomings in reliability, durability and stamina. Good streamlining, to use an old-fashioned phrase, originally came about not after development in a wind tunnel but after hard-pressed miles on the plains of Lombardy. The same testing under real road conditions helped prove the supplementary needs of proper seating, efficient controls and even decent ventilation. Add to these the propensity of the typical Italian driver to keep his right foot and the accelerator all the way to the floorboards at each and every opportunity and the end result is a breed of very good, tough, fast cars.

Unlike his German counterpart, the Italian fast car builder doesn't pay too much attention to the export of his products. The overseas sales effort made by Ferrari for instance cannot by any stretch of the imagination be compared to that of, say, Porsche. This *may* be due to the difference in production numbers of each marque but I am more inclined to the opinion

UCTION

that much of the answer lies in the character of each nationality. The Latin temperament holds sacred the knowledge that a Ferrari or a Maserati is so desirable that the rest of the world will beat a path to the gates of Maranello or Modena and beg to be allowed to buy one. German manufacturers are less inclined to such reticence, which may offer a crude explanation for the relative abundance of Porsches in, say, California, compared to a paucity of Ferraris.

This dogged determination on the part of German car makers to sell their products overseas, with proper back-up in the form of good dealers, extensive availability of spare parts and access to well trained technicians, not only contrasts with the Italian approach but also ensures that, in Germany, the profits from bigger sales can be ploughed back into research for the development of still better, faster cars.

These two differing attitudes can be well summed up in a comment I once heard from one of the most astute observers of the whole car business: 'To the Italian the production of a fast car is an art; to the German it is business'.

Of course, while most Germans regard their cars as simply functional, there are also those who love them with a fierce passion. One such is the owner of a chain of butchers shops in the Ruhr. He could afford to indulge in his particular dream car, based on a full-race Porsche 917, with a turbocharged flat-twelve engine which in its racing heyday was reputed to develop 1,200bhp! He wanted to use *his* 917 on the public roads, which meant that it had to be street-legalized, with new glass, different headlights, a quieter exhaust system, road tyres and dozens of other modifications to satisfy the law. He approached the Porsche factory to carry out these modifications but they declined — possibly fearing for his sanity! Undeterred, he asked one of the world's leading Porsche racing preparation companies to do the work. They were only too pleased to help and now, during the long summer months, he enjoys himself by driving the world's one and only street-legal Porsche 917!

This action might be considered wildly anti-social in most countries. In the USA for instance he might eventually have got the whole idea off the ground, but it would be hard to imagine such an enthusiast trying to stay on the right side of the law with a 230mph car on a 55mph highway. In Germany he was not only able to get the work done and make the car legal but he found that his neighbours, and seemingly every other road user, loved it! This example, extreme though it is, of the general attitude to the car in Germany, goes a long way to explaining why many people now think of Germany as the modern home of the fast car.

Germany certainly out-produces Italy in sheer numbers of fast cars per year, so if numbers alone mean anything Germany at least has a strong claim to that distinction — though as we will see, Italy and Germany, while undoubtedly the leading contenders, are by no means the only countries with a claim to stake. The USA, Japan, Britain, France — even Sweden and South Africa — build cars which qualify for inclusion in this exclusive league.

Finally, it is worth a moment to consider the future of the whole concept of the fast car. Italy has had speed limits on its superb network of autostradas for several years, yet fast cars are still rolling out of the Ferrari, Maserati, Lamborghini, and Fiat factories in greater numbers than ever before. There is little hope for the end of the USA's speed limit, but American manufacturers are turning back to a performance image. There are limits and legislation throughout Europe and Japan, but still the fast cars are launched, so maybe the imposition of speed limits and other regulations has no real effect. Even in de-restricted Germany it is rumoured that an 80mph speed limit could very soon be in operation. It is already being discussed at length, but knowing a little of the German character, I for one will believe it when I see it happen.

However they are marketed, there is no doubt that fast cars do still sell, even in situations where it would appear that every possible move has been made to restrict their sale and use. It was recently confirmed, for example, that the US national speed limit of 55mph (in force since 1975) would not be raised to a level more in line with modern cars and conditions, although all the evidence suggests that the restriction doesn't save any appreciable amount of fuel, or even lives. It simply makes life unnecessarily difficult for road users and for law enforcement authorities alike.

Yet the sales of really fast cars in the USA increase every year. In California, a state with arguably the best Highway Patrol authority of any and with one of the most anti-car legislatures of all, sales of Porsches have reached such a level that the marque seems almost as prevalent as the VW Beetle once was!

Whatever the future holds for the fast car as a breed, there are more really fast cars available today than at any other time in the history of motoring and now is the time to look at a stunning collection of them.

GERMANY

The German claim to be the true home of the fast car rests on much the same arguments as Italy's. The *autobahn* idea was originally tried during the 1920s, and not, as many people believe, only after Hitler came to power in 1933. An inner-city motorway, the Avus autobahn, was opened in Berlin in 1921 and, surprisingly, the German railway system built a section of autobahn near Bonn in 1928 for use by the public. The success of these early experiments showed Hitler that such a fast road system was feasible, cost effective and, for the military machine that he was building, vital for the rapid deployment of men, materials and equipment.

Since the turn of the century the German education system has placed great emphasis on technical training and research. The automobile received proper attention, fittingly so in the country of its real origin, and this was reinforced by the nature of the people who designed and built German cars. Among them are numbered innovative personalities like Gottlieb Daimler, Karl Benz, Ferdinand Porsche (who was actually an Austrian) and Felix Wankel. These men brought to their automotive genius that special Teutonic stubbornness recognized in so many aspects of German life, a special ability to grind away at problems until they have been surmounted, even if it should take years of effort.

I first noticed this characteristic during the first of many contacts with the Daimler-Benz company in Stuttgart. During 1967, I was taking photographs in the Untertürkheim factory and being shown around by one of the management. I commented on the high proportion of hand-finishing work in the typical Mercedes-Benz car compared to its nearest British counterpart and on the workers' obviously intense application to their work. The whole factory was literally humming with effort. I was quietly informed that the company knew exactly what was expected from everyone involved with the production of its cars and if that meant, for instance, a 30% increase in the inspection staff then that was what happened. The executive went on to describe the Swabian worker as the best in the world, especially for car manufacture; hard working, loyal, self critical and determined to make the best car possible. There was a degree of arrogance in his attitude but it was a benign arrogance, very much like that to be found at Rolls-Royce! In fact it is actually pride, a feature common to all great engineers whatever their nationality.

Germans do not particularly expect life to be easy (although this attitude has begun to change in the last few years) but in my own experience the majority of Germans take life, work and pleasure very seriously. They work hard at all of them! Efficiency is the path they follow and when it comes to making a fast car they make that too as efficient as they can. Each major German manufacturer approaches this important task in his own way as can be seen later.

One final, vital factor, at least over the last 30 years, that has created Germany's present strength as a car manufacturer is its willingness to reinvest profits in research and

development. The German industry has shown that it will pay top salaries for top men and these are the sort of men who help Germany produce world beating cars. The German driver works his car hard and expects total reliability, which has made sure that only the most durable of cars succeeds in this very demanding market place.

I have already offered reasons why Germany might justifiably consider itself to be today's real home of the fast car. In this chapter I will begin to look at the cars themselves and describe a selection of the fastest German production models and their capabilities.

At the time of writing there are no fewer than 35 different models available from German manufacturers which will exceed the base-line 125mph. Most are available in all European markets and in the USA, but specifications — even availability — do vary with local requirements and most of these descriptions will be based on home market models, which are, of course, the most typical.

In West Germany there aren't any speed limits on *Autobahnen* (motorways) so it's one of the few places in the world where you can test those top speed figures for yourself. Maybe that's why German makers can still justify small volume performance models like the Volkswagen Corrado (above) and the Porsche 911 Speedster (left).

PORSCHE

PORSCHE 959

Porsche have the unique distinction among the major German makers of being able to claim that all its models will exceed 125mph! Where better to start then, than with a look at the fastest Porsche model of them all, the 959. This first went on sale in 1985, in a strictly limited edition — at a price (at the time) equivalent to twice that of a Ferrari 512BB or Aston Martin Vantage in both the USA and Great Britain. All the cars have now been sold, and they were all ordered well ahead of the date when they were built. Three versions were offered: the basic one, with a luxurious interior, was the cheapest, while the price for the sporting competition version and the ultimate racing version went up in ever higher leaps and bounds.

The technical specification of the 959 would not be out of place on a NASA space project. Its body is made of Kevlar, a material more usually found in the bodies of endurance racing or Grand Prix cars. This immensely strong, light and corrosion-resistant material has been formed into a wind-cheating shape with a very impressive aerodynamic drag coefficient, or Cd, of only 0·32 yet weighing only 1,226·5lb. The 959's styling continues the recognizable Porsche theme that can be traced back to the introduction of the 356 series, over 35 years ago. In the writer's eyes it is one of the best looking of all Porsches. The Kevlar body is mounted on a galvanized steel chassis that carries racing type suspension with dual wishbones at front and rear. Twin dampers are fitted all round, and those at the front incorporate dual springs. The driver can adjust both ride height and spring rates from the cockpit even while the car is on the move.

On the 959, Porsche fit magnesium wheels with hollow spokes, which allow the wheel and tyre assembly to be monitored constantly for punctures or structural failure. Not only will a drop in tyre pressure due to a puncture be registered but any crack in the wheel material will also cause a loss of pressure and can also be noted instantly by the driver. The tyres are secured to the wheel rims and in the event of a puncture should give the driver time to slow and stop the 959 with complete safety.

The four-wheel-drive system is electronically controlled, to give optimum traction to the car by varying the front-to-rear drive balance automatically at all road speeds. In typically Porsche fashion this fail-safe arrangement has a manual override to allow the driver to select his own setup should he feel that conditions warrant it.

The mid-engined 959 uses a refinement of Porsche's existing 935/936 racing engines that have been so successful throughout the world in recent years. It is a twin turbocharged 2.85-litre flat-six unit with an intercooler. The cylinder heads feature four valves per cylinder and water cooling. The engine block itself however is air cooled. This engine's power output is rated at a minimum of 400bhp and the 959 will accelerate

The 959 is the fastest and most expensive car Porsche have ever offered for the road. Although the shape is clearly related to the 911, the car owes more allegiance to the 935 racers.

SPECIFICATION	
MODEL/TYPE	PORSCHE 959
ENGINE	FLAT-6, 2,850CC, TURBO
HORSEPOWER	400BHP PLUS
TRANSMISSION	6-SPEED 4-WD
CHASSIS	KEVLAR/STEEL
BRAKES	4-WHEEL DISC
TOP SPEED	190MPH PLUS
ACCELERATION 0–100MPH	UNDER 8 SECS
PRODUCTION SPAN	1985–87

from zero to 62mph in 4.9 seconds, with a top speed of over 190mph! As with all previous Porsche engines the unit has enormous potential for further development in terms of both performance and refinement, and over the next few years will undoubtedly reach quite staggering power outputs.

Porsche built only 200 examples of the car, with a further 20 pure competition models prepared for racing by the factory and selected private teams. The car's aspirations as a top class rally car were scotched, however, when the Group B class was deemed too fast and dangerous!

PORSCHE

PORSCHE 911 TURBO

In descending order of performance the Porsche line-up continues with the 911 Turbo model, which is known as the 930 in North America. This car can accurately be described as the current ultimate expression of the 911 concept, that was introduced way back in late 1964. Progressive improvements over the years have upped the 911's power output from 130bhp to 300bhp! Any doubts, however, as to whether the 911 chassis could really cope with 300bhp had already been allayed by even more powerful racing derivatives and the 911 Turbo has all the necessary refinements to enable it to handle this massive amount of power with ease.

Nevertheless, experience suggests that only a really capable driver, used to handling large numbers of horses, can utilize the remarkable potential of this machine to the full. Over the years, together with the substantial power increases, Porsche have improved the roadholding of their rear-engined cars to the extent that now even with so much horsepower it is both easier and safer to use all the available performance. However, in the case of the 911 Turbo in particular, it would be a very foolish driver indeed, especially on wet, twisty roads, who did not treat his car with a deal of respect. Full throttle in the middle of a wet corner is a sure recipe for landing in the ditch!

Like all the 911 models, the Turbo retains some aspects from its past, in particular, its instruments and heating. As with all air-cooled cars the efficiency of the 911's heating and ventilation system varies with the engine speed — slow running in traffic means that little heat is supplied but fast, high-revs use supplies almost too much heat and finding the best compromise is not easy. The instrumentation of the 911 series lags behind the best examples of today's cars; with the exception of the speedo and rev-counter, the other dials and switches are scattered about the dash, and to a new driver they do not fall to hand easily.

A Porsche, however, is not just about decent heating and instrument layout, it is about quality of construction, value for money, sheer performance and fun. The 911 Turbo may be flawed, but its virtues outweigh its faults by a very wide margin. A top speed of over 160mph, acceleration from zero to 62mph in just 5·4 seconds, fuel consumption of 23·9mpg at a steady 75mph, together with the car's incredibly stable resale value really do put the Porsche 911 Turbo into a very special category.

Although introduced as long ago as 1975 and based on a series which dates from 1964, the Porsche 911 Turbo is still the fastest accelerating car of any in series production. Its understated, almost mundane looks belie truly stunning performance. Porsche pioneered the use of aerodynamic wings on road cars and, with a car as quick as the Turbo, they are not simply for show.

SPECIFICATION	
MODEL/TYPE	PORSCHE 911 TURBO
ENGINE	FLAT-6, 3,299CC, TURBO
HORSEPOWER	300BHP @ 5,500RPM
TRANSMISSION	4-SPEED MANUAL
CHASSIS	STEEL MONOCOQUE
BRAKES	4-WHEEL DISC
TOP SPEED	160MPH
ACCELERATION 0–60MPH	5.4 SECS
PRODUCTION SPAN	1981 →

PORSCHE

PORSCHE 911 CS

For about two-thirds of the price of a Turbo there is a Porsche which, to my mind, offers even better value for money. It is the 911 Carrera Sport, with a top speed only about 10mph down on that of the Turbo, at 152mph, better fuel economy, with 31·4mpg at 75mph and a slightly longer 0–62mph acceleration time of 6·1 seconds. The Carrera Sport is more drivable in all conditions than the Turbo, being less nervous in its manner of going. Its five-speed gearbox (compared to the Turbo's four-speed unit) gives a better spread of ratios, and the car feels better balanced on its recently improved suspension. This Porsche model must be *the* car to lay away, like a good wine, except that it is so much fun to use that it would be very difficult to put it into storage.

Like its predecessor, the 1973 911 Carrera, the very latest version is an instant classic of its type. Some time ago I drove from Los Angeles to New York in a factory prepared Carrera. By comparison with today's car its suspension was firm to the point of being harsh, there was a complete lack of body sound damping, so the car was pretty noisy, but oh, how it went! Crossing Kansas I came across a 47-mile straight road, an empty road, devoid of traffic, people, even birds. I opened up the Porsche and ran flat out for the whole length of that road. The speedometer needle went right off the scale, at 160mph, and stayed there, speeding up on the down slopes, holding the speed on the upgrades and flat sections. The Carrera was as stable as could be; the steering remained positive, without any suggestion of lightness and at the end of the long straight the brakes came on with complete conviction, stopping the car without drama.

You could never say that the Porsche 911 CS range of supercars wasn't diverse: the ultra high-performance CS Carrera (below) is just a step away from the fire-breathing Turbo in the 'go' stakes while the Carrera cabriolet (right) offers svelte, open-air fun. The Targa (below, left) is perhaps the most versatile, with its detachable roof panel.

S P E C I F I C A T I O N	
MODEL/TYPE	PORSCHE 911 CS
ENGINE	FLAT-6, 3,164CC, OHC
HORSEPOWER	231BHP @ 5,900RPM
TRANSMISSION	5-SPEED MANUAL
CHASSIS	STEEL MONOCOQUE
BRAKES	4-WHEEL DISC
TOP SPEED	152MPH
ACCELERATION 0–60MPH	6.1 SECS
PRODUCTION SPAN	1984 →

PORSCHE

PORSCHE 928S

After the introduction of the 924 model in 1975, rumours soon began to circulate that it would not be long before Porsche would bring out a super-sports coupé, incorporating all that they had learnt with this, their first front-engined car. Enthusiasts were not to be disappointed, as the new 928 broke fresh ground for Porsche.

All previous Porsche cars except the 924 had been either rear-engined or mid-engined, so the 928 was a new departure with its front-mounted V8. This engine featured an alloy block with the pistons running directly in the cylinder bores without the usual benefit of steel liners, and hydraulic tappets. The 928 also offered the option of an automatic gearbox, made by Daimler-Benz. Like the standard five-speed manual transmission, this unit as used on the 928 was located at the rear of the car in unit with the differential. This feature (which was shared by the 924) provided the 928 with near perfect 50/50 front-to-rear balance, with obvious benefits in ride, handling and braking.

Early road test comments waxed lyrical over the car, its performance and its overall dynamic qualities but suggested that an anti-lock braking system (ABS) could well be applied to the 928 and more performance would not be unwelcome. They also, in the main, went on to declare the automatic gearbox as much better suited to the 928 than the manual component, as it appeared to match the character of the car so perfectly — a surprising comment perhaps, in view of the very sporting nature of Porsche products.

With the S model which followed soon after, and today's 928S Series 4, it would appear that the original criticisms, minor though they were, have been dealt with. Now, the 928S is generally regarded as one of the very best two-seater high performance cars of all time. Many ordinarily cynical road-testers have gone into raptures over the car, their only criticism being that their bank balance wouldn't allow them to

SPECIFICATION	
MODEL/TYPE	PORSCHE 928S
ENGINE	V8, 4,957CC, SOHC
HORSEPOWER	310BHP @ 5,900RPM
TRANSMISSION	5-SP/4-SP AUTO
CHASSIS	STEEL MONOCOQUE
BRAKES	4-WHEEL DISC
TOP SPEED	164MPH
ACCELERATION 0–60MPH	5.9 SECS
PRODUCTION SPAN	1987→

The 928S is widely regarded as a 'softer' Porsche although the 911 types make most cars look relatively tame. The 928 is just different, a great state-of-the-art car in its own right, largely free of the 911's aggressive image.

own one!

Technical details of the 928S Series 4 give some idea of the immense care and attention to detail that Porsche lavish in ensuring that lovers of fast cars continue to feel this way about the model. The fuel-injected engine has a compression ratio of 10.0:1 to give excellent thermodynamic efficiency with low fuel consumption and the car's superb aerodynamic shape helps in achieving consumption figures of 25.9mpg at 75mph, even with the four-speed automatic 'box. A peak of 320bhp is developed at 6000rpm. The 0–60 time is a very quick 5.9 seconds and the top speed is 164mph. The Porsche 928S Series 4 is a very fine automobile, albeit a rather expensive one, but ownership costs are reduced to quite reasonable levels largely because the servicing intervals are now 12,000 miles.

PORSCHE

PORSCHE 944 TURBO

Early in 1985 Porsche announced its latest high performance car, the long-awaited 944 Turbo model. The body styling is very little different from the non-turbo 944 and the car is priced between the 911 Carerra on the one hand and the 911 Turbo on the other. The 944 Turbo's front-mounted four-cylinder engine produces 250bhp, enough to propel the car to a top speed of 153mph and cover the 0–60mph run in just 6 seconds. Fuel consumption is, overall, 22.9mpg, just about bettering that of the 911 Carrera. The car's turbocharger is water-cooled and both an intercooler and an engine oil cooler are fitted, displaying again the attention to detail which is a feature of the Porsche way of doing things.

The improvement in performance over the standard 944 can be quickly gauged if you compare the top speed of 136mph, 0–60mph in 7 seconds for the 'ordinary' car, and the very similar fuel economy, which helps to balance the substantial difference in price. On each model of 944 certain common features remain: low-drag aerodynamics, a good balance between performance and fuel economy, high top speed, good handling, steering and braking, remarkably high levels of build, fit and finish — together with an understated appearance that appeals to the appreciative enthusiast.

The Porsche 944 successfully filled the void between the relatively low-powered 924 and the more 'serious' 911 and 928 models, when it was introduced in 1982. The shape of the basic coupé (above and below) has remained little altered, but a new convertible (right) should help to widen the appeal of this 'entry-level' Porsche.

S P E C I F I C A T I O N	
MODEL/TYPE	**PORSCHE 944 TURBO**
ENGINE	**4-CYL, 2,479CC, TURBO**
HORSEPOWER	**250BHP @ 6,000RPM**
TRANSMISSION	**5-SPEED MANUAL**
CHASSIS	**STEEL MONOCOQUE**
BRAKES	**4-WHEEL DISC**
TOP SPEED	**153MPH**
ACCELERATION 0–60MPH	**6 SECS**
PRODUCTION SPAN	**1985 →**

BMW

BMW 850i

When the BMW 635 Series cars were discontinued in favour of the new 850 in early 1990, a 13 year tradition was broken. The 635s had grown into mature sporting coupés, extremely well engineered and built, combining the best of all worlds for drivers with high expectations.

The BMW 850i has, therefore, a hard act to follow. While its outward appearance has been criticised for looking too much like a Japanese offering, with a bland, flat front swooping nose section, the sparkling V12 5-litre BMW unit is one of the best engines of all time.

The 850i is an occasional 2+2, although great care has gone into the interior design to ensure easy access to the rear quarters. The front instrument console sweeps between driver and passenger, placing each in a luxuriously trimmed cocoon. Under the bonnet the silk smooth V12 can effortlessly propel the coupé to a regulated 155mph at a moderate 5,200rpm. The 0–60mph dash is achieved in 7.4 seconds although, when a manual box becomes available, this figure should drop well below 7 seconds. German speed regulation agreements prevent the 850i reaching its full potential, and a six-speed manual box could take the car to 179mph – in theory of course. A Cd of 0.29 is not hampered by the twin pop-up lamps emerging from the front end of the bonnet, and overall aerodynamics are far more slippery than the old 635.

At the rear end BMW's revolutionary five-link suspension keeps the 235/50 ZR16 Pirellis glued to the road, while at the front the experienced 750i front suspension set-up knows well how to cope with the V12 bulk above it.

BMW's new 850i coupé combines the performance of a supercar – with its V12 power – and the traditional luxury and executive appeal you can find in the Munich company's other cars.

SPECIFICATION	
MODEL/TYPE	BMW 850i
ENGINE	V12-Cyl, 4,988CC
HORSEPOWER	300BHP @ 5,200RPM
TRANSMISSION	4-SP AUTO/6-SP MANUAL (OPTION)
CHASSIS	STEEL MONOCOQUE
BRAKES	4-WHEEL DISC
TOP SPEED	155MPH (REGULATED)
ACCELERATION 0–60MPH	7.4 SECS
PRODUCTION SPAN	1990 →

BMW

BMW M635CSi

The current top of the league among BMW's performance cars is the M635CSi coupé. This new model has recently received a series of major improvements over the previous, and already excellent, 635CSi machine. The new in-line 3,453cc six-cylinder engine has duplex-chain-driven double overhead cams, four valves per cylinder and a compression ratio raised to 9.6:1, instead of the previous 9.3:1. Maximum power is now 286bhp but the new engine is both lighter and more fuel efficient than the earlier unit. At 75mph, consumption is 32.1mpg for the manual gearbox version, which is a remarkable figure. Digital engine electronics controlling the ignition and fuel supply systems have been programmed to give optimum timing and fuel metering under all conditions of speed, engine temperature, air temperature, barometric pressure and other variables. For such a large car with this kind of performance the M635CSi's paltry appetite for fuel is astonishing.

An ABS, anti-lock braking system, is fitted as standard, increasing the braking performance of the car and allowing it to be utilized at maximum efficiency while retaining full steering effect at the same time.

One particularly interesting feature of all the big BMWs is the availability of the ZF four-speed automatic gearbox, with its three ranges of operation. With this unit, a small switch selects either 'E', for economy, wherein the car assumes a high set of overall ratios, giving excellent fuel consumption but slightly slower acceleration, 'S' for sports-type driving, where there is a change to a lower set of overall ratios for more rapid acceleration, and a third position allowing the gearbox to be used effectively as a manual transmission. With this gearbox, the M635CSi can improve on its fuel consumption figures quite appreciably, to register 32.5mpg at a steady 75mph and no less than 41.5mpg at 56mph, while top speed is 158mph!

The big BMW coupé is smooth, so very smooth to drive — quiet and comfortable enough for four large adults to cover hundreds of miles in a day and not feel distressed at the end of the journey. The BMW's steering and braking are more than capable of handling any road situation, and even visibility for the driver, often a bugbear with coupés, is excellent. Heating, which used to be less than good, is now very much improved, as is the ventilation system. For customers who have to have four decent seats in their coupé, plus all the dash and glamour of a really fast car there is not much that can hold a candle to the M635CSi BMW. At a price, close to, say, a Porsche 928S or a Ferrari Mondial, it is out on its own as a four-seater — nothing else even comes close to its combination of comfort, safety, style and performance.

The ultimate driving machine? BMW Motorsport division's engine and suspension modifications turn the already rapid 635CSi into the incredible M635CSi (below). The heart of the matter is a 286bhp 24-valve version of the superb BMW straight-six engine (below right). The 635CSP (far right) is a limited edition 6 Series coupé to help keep interest in the car alive after the 850i's launch.

S P E C I F I C A T I O N	
MODEL/TYPE	BMW M635CSi
ENGINE	6-CYL, 3,453CC, SOHC
HORSEPOWER	286BHP
TRANSMISSION	5-SPEED MANUAL
CHASSIS	STEEL MONOCOQUE
BRAKES	4-WHEEL DISC
TOP SPEED	158MPH
ACCELERATION 0–60MPH	6 SECS
PRODUCTION SPAN	1984 →

BMW M535i

The old BMW 5 Series was looking distinctly aged when it was replaced in 1988 — not surprisingly, really, as the car was introduced as long ago as 1972. The brand new 5 Series is as sleek and modern as the old one was sharp and dated, and there are four engines to choose from — 2-litre, 2.5-litre, 3-litre and 3.5-litre — and each model is available with an SE (special equipment) package. The ultimate version is, therefore, the 535iSE.

The similarity between the new 5 Series and the 7 Series is no coincidence — the two shapes were developed side-by-side — and it's a very clean shape, with a low nose and high tail with an integral spoiler. Aerodynamics are drastically improved and the new car's drag co-efficient, at 0.32, is an 18 per cent improvement on that of the outgoing model. The car continues the BMW tradition for drivers' cars, with a close-ratio five-speed gearbox, together with anti-lock brakes, an Automatic Stability Control and Electronic Damper Control to allay any fears about wet-weather skittishness. Top speed is a pulse-raising 141mph while 60mph is reached in a mere 7.4 seconds. Near 50-50 weight distribution and an ideal ride/handling compromise mean that the 535i is a brilliant long-distance sports saloon. One criticism: space in the back is not generous.

SPECIFICATION	
MODEL/TYPE	BMW 535i
ENGINE	6-Cyl, 3,430CC, 50 HC
HORSEPOWER	211BHP
TRANSMISSION	5-SPEED/4-SPEED AUTO
CHASSIS	STEEL MONOCOQUE
BRAKES	4-WHEEL DISC
TOP SPEED	141MPH
ACCELERATION 0–60MPH	7.4 SECS
PRODUCTION SPAN	1988 →

BMW's new 5 Series has buried for ever the staid image that the old range had established, with smooth new styling and the type of 'junior' executive car kudos that Jaguar won in the 1960s with its Mk 2 saloon . . . but where's Jaguar's challenger now?

5 SERIES
5 SERIES

ALPINA BMW B10

The Alpina B10 cars are based on the current BMW 5 Series cars, the 535i or 535i Sport. The Alpina package provides the 5 Series owner with an uprated superbly engineered pace car, more than just another tuned BMW.

Alpina, the most respected of the many companies which tune and otherwise modify BMWs, is based in the village of Buchloe – not far from BMW's own headquarters in Munich.

The company was established in 1965 by Burkard Bovensiepen, a large, amiable man who is a wine connoisseur as well as being a car manufacturer – the only car manufacturer in the world sanctioned by BMW to produce versions of its cars, sold worldwide as Alpina BMWs. For many years, Alpina and BMW have co-operated closely in developing both road and racing cars, with many impressive wins including the prestigious European Touring car Championship.

Unlike most, Alpina do not simply bolt on more engine power, but completely re-engineer the basic car with modified suspension, brakes, aerodynamics and interior fittings. Alpina offer virtually any level of modification desired on any of BMW's range of cars and the 5 Series based B10 is just the latest in a long line of successful cars.

The B10's powerplant is an in-line six cylinder 3,430cc unit, which is capable of producing 260bhp at 5,700rpm. Maximum torque of 330 Nm occurs at 4,000rpm. The seven bearing crank, light Mahle cast pistons, light alloy cylinder head, complete with hemispherical combustion chambers all add up to an exciting engine package. Alpina engines are tested thoroughly before they are offered to the public and all technical aspects of the car are evaluated and where necessary, modified. Alpina fit their own large bore exhaust system for instance. Suspension is another area where detailed modifications are carried out. The B10 features Alpina devised Bilstein gas filled shock absorbers, and suspension springs. Transmission of all that extra power makes its way to the rear wheels via a special Alpina limited slip differential.

Visually, Alpina cars can be distinguished by deeper spoilers striking light alloy wheels and fatter Michelin MXX rubber covers.

But it's the performance figures which tell the Alpina story best. The 0–100 Km/h dash is achieved in 6.5 seconds, the standing start kilometre in 27.9 seconds, and a magnificently swift top speed of 156mph rounds off this impressive array.

Standard BMWs offer enough performance and style for most but for those who want added punch and meaner looks than Alpina's versions, like this B10, fit the bill.

S P E C I F I C A T I O N	
MODEL/TYPE	**ALPINA BMW B10**
ENGINE	**6-Cyl, 3,430CC, SOHC**
HORSEPOWER	**260BHP @ 5,700RPM**
TRANSMISSION	**5-SPEED/4-SPEED AUTO**
CHASSIS	**STEEL MONOCOQUE**
BRAKES	**4-WHEEL DISC**
TOP SPEED	**156MPH**
ACCELERATION 0–60MPH	**6.5 SECS**
PRODUCTION SPAN	**1989 →**

BMW

BMW 750iL

At a stroke BMW produced what many think is the world's best executive saloon – the new 7 Series. The standard car is enough for most but BMW-recognised tuner Alpina can soup it up for you (right), while BMW's own and magnificent V12-engined 750iL (below) has revived interest in 12-cylinder cars.

During the dark years of seventies fuel crises and cash-starvation for most motor manufacturers to develop high performance cars, V12 engines were few and far between; for many years just Jaguar and Ferrari offered the cylinder configuration in their cars, Jaguar in the XJ12 and XJS coupé, Ferrari in its big, front-engined 400 and 412.

But in post depression nineties times, the major makers of executive cars and supercars – including Jaguar, BMW, Mercedes-Benz, Porsche and Cadillac – are fighting a pitch battle for a slice of this expanding and lucrative market. It was in this market climate that BMW's first V12 engine saw the light of day.

So far it's only available in one model — the 750iL, the top 7 Series car and the flagship of BMW's fleet. The engine, with its head cast in silicon aluminium and with a single overhead camshaft, chain-driven to each bank of six cylinders, is an incredible sight to behold beneath the sleek bonnet of the top 7, and the power it puts out, some 300bhp at 5200rpm, is enough to push the car's top speed to 158mph; that precise figure is so because the Bavarian company has chosen to fit a speed limiter to the engine, and there is little doubt that the car would go a good deal faster if it wasn't specified — faster still in a lighter chassis — because the 750iL is a very heavy car at 4233lb. The 750iL is 4½in longer than other models in the 7 Series — the 730 and 735i — although a standard wheelbase edition is available. Other differences are wider BMW 'kidney' grilles at the front and a buffalo hide-trimmed interior.

SPECIFICATION	
MODEL/TYPE	BMW 750iL
ENGINE	V12, 4,988CC, SOHC
HORSEPOWER	300BHP
TRANSMISSION	4-SPEED AUTO
CHASSIS	STEEL MONOCOQUE
BRAKES	4-WHEEL DISC
TOP SPEED	158MPH
ACCELERATION 0–60MPH	7.7 SECS
PRODUCTION SPAN	1987 →

MERCEDES-BENZ

Turning to the fastest cars from Mercedes-Benz themselves, however, I must admit to a sneaking regard for the products. Over the last 15 years I have had a professional relationship with the company, and never fail to be impressed when I drive their cars. At the same time, however, I must admit that I have yet to own one! The reason is strictly personal. I actually find it difficult to be enthusiastic about perfection, when, as in the case of Mercedes-Benz cars, it translates to a clinical coldness, an unappealing machine-like efficiency. There is no denying, however, that Mercedes-Benz cars are among the best mass-produced cars available in the world today.

I have selected three cars from Untertürkheim to represent Mercedes-Benz and these are the 560SEC, 560SEL and the 500SL.

With its elegant 380SEC coupé (right) and 560SEC coupé (below) Mercedes-Benz show that it is possible to combine performance with style and still retain a strong marque identity – even though the functional simplicity which characterizes the marque is interpreted by some as blandness.

MERCEDES-BENZ 560SEC

The 560SEC is a superb four-seater coupé, well able to carry four adults far and fast, with excellent economy of operation. Its 5547cc V8 engine produces 300bhp at 5000rpm, and 335lb ft of torque at 3750rpm. Maximum speed is 156mph and the 560SEC can maintain this speed all day if necessary! Its 0–60mph time is very good, at 8 seconds, but the overall fuel consumption is only average, at 26.9mpg. In appearance the 560SEC rivals the very good looks of the BMW635CSi and is without doubt one of the most handsome Mercedes-Benz cars ever made.

In my eyes, the 560SEC is so good-looking that anyone thinking about adding any of the increasingly prevalent after-market body styling appendages should really think very carefully before changing the standard car's beautifully balanced appearance.

SPECIFICATION	
MODEL/TYPE	MERCEDES-BENZ 560SEC
ENGINE	V8, 5,547CC, DOHC
HORSEPOWER	300BHP @ 5,000RPM
TRANSMISSION	4-SPEED AUTO
CHASSIS	STEEL MONOCOQUE
BRAKES	4-WHEEL DISC
TOP SPEED	156MPH
ACCELERATION 0–60MPH	8 SECS
PRODUCTION SPAN	1986→

MERCEDES-BENZ

MERCEDES-BENZ 560SEL

The 560SEL is the most expensive Mercedes 'S' saloon, using a 5547cc V8 engine, producing 300bhp at 5000rpm, which gives the 3991lb car a top speed of 156mph. The 'S-class' Mercedes-Benz has been one of the most desirable mass produced cars of recent years and the longer-bodied SEL is even more admirable in all respects.

Until the S-class cars came along I thought Mercedes-Benz were without a really good looking model in their range but with the S cars all that has changed. Having looked closely at a number of body styling exercises on Mercedes-Benz models over the last two years I still think that the standard shape is unequalled for looks and proportions.

Fuel consumption for the 560SEL is bound not to be sparing, but this lengthy car gives 26.9mpg and for such a large car it is surprisingly easy to drive quickly. It appears to shrink as the miles fly past, allowing the driver to place the car very accurately on corners. Brakes are discs all round, those at the front are internally ventilated and ABS comes as standard. The transmission is the excellent Mercedes-Benz four-speed automatic and the differential is a limited-slip unit. Suspension is independent all round, with the front having anti-dive characteristics and the rear incorporating anti-squat control.

Mercedes-Benz seats may provide rather a surprise to most people sitting in one of these cars for the first time, as they appear to be both plain and very hard! However, they are anatomically correct in their design and very comfortable even over very long distances. A trip from Nairobi to Mombasa, for instance, through the Tsavo Game Park, over rutted murram tracks in a 280SE left the author feeling no worse than a drive across town.

Irrespective of performance and price, the 560SEL is one of today's great automobiles.

SPECIFICATION	
MODEL/TYPE	MERCEDES-BENZ 560SEL
ENGINE	V8, 5,547CC, DOHC
HORSEPOWER	300BHP @ 5,000RPM
TRANSMISSION	4-SPEED AUTO
CHASSIS	STEEL MONOCOQUE
BRAKES	4-WHEEL DISC
TOP SPEED	156MPH
ACCELERATION 0–60MPH	7.1 SECS
PRODUCTION SPAN	1986→

MERCEDES-BENZ

MERCEDES-BENZ 500SL

It came second in the 1989 Car of the Year awards and the waiting list stretches far into the future for Mercedes-Benz's fabulous new SL sports cars. Every one comes with its own hardtop (top right), while the car's roll-bar pops up (below) in the event of a roll-over accident or when the car experiences serious G-forces.

Mercedes-Benz' brand new SL range of roadsters promises to continue a tradition for svelte, sophisticated, and civilised rather than raucous sports cars that began with the 300 and 190SL roadsters of the fifties. The out-going range, introduced in 1971, has continued to sell bouyantly right up to this day.

Top model in the new, smoothly-styled range is the 500SL, which comes with a four-valves-per-cylinder version of the well-known Mercedes V8 engine, rated at 4973cc and giving out a massive 326bhp at 5500rpm — the 5-litre motor of the old car 'only' gave 265bhp. This should be good for 155mph. But there is more to come — Mercedes plans to rival BMW and Jaguar with the launch of its very own V12 engine within a couple of years although it will be governed not to exceed 155mph either.

The beautiful styling of the new SL roadster is set to take it well into the nineties and a novel feature is a concealed roll-over bar that will automatically appear — within a third of a second — in the event of the car turning over.

SPECIFICATION	
MODEL/TYPE	MERCEDES-BENZ 500SL
ENGINE	V8, 4,973CC, DOHC
HORSEPOWER	326BHP @ 5,500RPM
TRANSMISSION	4-SPEED AUTO
CHASSIS	STEEL MONOCOQUE
BRAKES	4-WHEEL DISC
TOP SPEED	155MPH
ACCELERATION 0–60MPH	6.2 SECS
PRODUCTION SPAN	1989→

S SL 500

AUDI

For many years, Audi made low priced, sensible cars, for the family that aspired to a BMW but couldn't afford one. They were well made in the German manner, rather lacking in character but making up for that by being so well put together and finished. Gradually, Audi's cars became bigger, faster and more sought after by an increasingly prosperous middle class in Europe.

Ten years ago the drive from Cologne to Frankfurt could be undertaken in just under two hours but it took an expensive, fast car to do it. I recently did the same journey in an Audi 80CD and very comfortably took 25 minutes off that time. As a practical measure of the improvement in the current crop of everyday cars this sort of comparison of journey times is of more value than any test track measurement.

Currently there are six Audi cars that can easily exceed 125mph, the 100CD, 200ST, 200T, Quattro, 200 Quattro and now the Quattro Sport. They are all excellent cars but I have zeroed in on the fastest, the 155mph Quattro Sport, not only because it *is* the fastest but also because it incorporates all the latest technology coming out of Audi's base at Ingolstadt. It is also the most expensive car Audi has ever offered to the public, if only a very limited public!

AUDI QUATTRO SPORT

The Audi Sport's capabilities take it out of the merely fast into the super-fast, super-expensive class of car, although it has more than a passing similarity to the more mundane Audi GT coupé. By no means a beautiful car, some have labelled the Sport downright ugly. It sits on a wheelbase that is two inches shorter than that of an Austin Rover Metro, giving the car a short, squat appearance, emphasized by a longer nose to accommodate the intercooler for the turbo unit.

The engine, a new five-cylinder unit, is a benchmark for any turbo installation and marks another step in the progress of

SPECIFICATION	
MODEL/TYPE	AUDI QUATTRO SPORT
ENGINE	5-CYL, 2,133CC, TURBO
HORSEPOWER	300BHP @ 6,500RPM
TRANSMISSION	5-SPEED MANUAL
CHASSIS	STEEL/GRP/KEVLAR
BRAKES	4-WHEEL DISC
TOP SPEED	155MPH
ACCELERATION 0–60MPH	5 SECS
PRODUCTION SPAN	1985–86

extracting usable power by means of the exhaust-driven blower. After the introduction of this engine, Audi upped its power in 1980 from 115bhp on carburettors to 130bhp using fuel injection. Use of the turbocharger increased this to 200bhp, with the works rally cars enjoying the benefits of up to 350bhp. This car delivers a reliable 300bhp at 6500rpm even in standard form. Current rally cars have 450bhp, with another 50bhp to come for next year.

The engine installation in the Quattro Sport represents the fourth generation of Audi turbo refinement with its twin overhead camshafts operating four valves per cylinder. The engine, in alloy, is nearly 50lb lighter than the previous cast iron-block engine and is the first all-alloy Audi engine to be offered to the public.

The interior may *promise* to be able to accommodate four people, but in practice the Sport is strictly a two-seater and

AUDI

there is no way that even two small children can be carried in comfort on the rear seats. The body, which is made by Baur, has boot and roof sections of aluminium reinforced glassfibre, with other body parts using Kevlar material.

One very distinct difference from other Audi models is that the Sport must have the aerodynamic qualities of a house brick, yet sitting on its 225/50VR 15 Pirelli P7 tyres the Sport has all the charisma of the Ferrari GTO.

Never noted as the smoothest of engines, the 2,133cc five-cylinder Audi unit in its latest guise is surprisingly silky, almost as smooth as a BMW six. Real power starts to come in at over 3,000rpm when the familiar turbo 'whoosh', sounding like an astonished gasp from an unsuspecting passenger, takes over. There is also some extra noise from the transmission but its shift quality is not affected and it remains smooth and positive. The brakes are ventilated discs all round and have selectable ABS anti-lock capability. Audi have found that ABS is not necessarily desirable in all driving conditions and in some circumstances can be dispensed with to advantage, so they give a Sport driver the option.

Ride quality is firmer than previous Quattros, to the point where it could almost be described as harsh but, if anything, the roadholding of this car is appreciably better. Steering is also improved to the point where the Sport is easier to drive really fast, much faster than the contemporary Quattro, and with greater relaxation.

Anyone with the equivalent of £60,000 to spend on a car, a two-seater remember, that is in the forefront of the latest technology, with the reliability and durability that comes from German engineering, and which is as safe as any car manufacturer can make it, should look no further than an Audi Quattro Sport.

The stubby and purposeful-looking Audi Quattro Sport (previous page) takes the four-wheel drive format of the original Quattro (below) a stage further, in a short-wheelbase derivative designed primarily (though not entirely successfully) for rallying.

B169 CRP

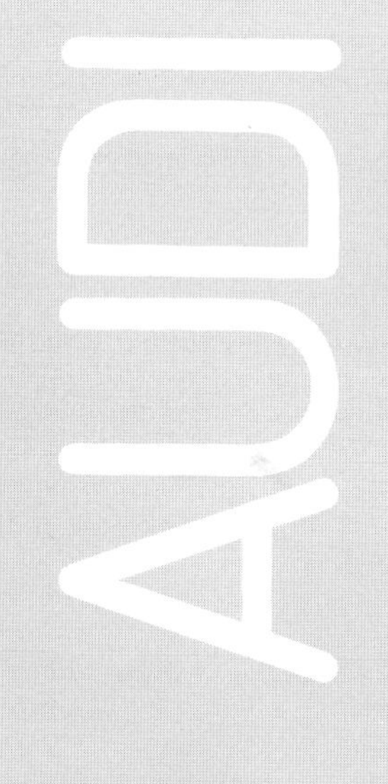

AUDI 2005T

For the fast car buyer who must have a full five-seater with all the basic advantages of an Audi, the Audi 2005T model may be an ideal choice. The larger 200 body style gives sumptuous accommodation for five large adults with every possible comfort, and the driver has near-sportscar performance to keep him happy. The 2005T has a top speed of 143mph, will accelerate from zero to 60mph in 8.2 seconds and offers overall fuel consumption of just over 19mpg — and this maker's quoted figure for top speed is probably more than a little on the conservative side. The beautifully finished Audi 2005T has only two small causes for criticism. Firstly, it is very expensive within its class and secondly it shares a characteristic with most other Audis of being too cold and clinical. That however is the price to be paid for a near perfect automobile. If I had to transport five adults a long way in a hurry and in considerable comfort then I can think of few better alternatives than the Audi 2005T.

SPECIFICATION	
MODEL/TYPE	AUDI 2005T
ENGINE	5-CYL, 2,144CC, SOHC
HORSEPOWER	182BHP @ 5,700RPM
TRANSMISSION	5-SPEED MANUAL
CHASSIS	STEEL MONOCOQUE
BRAKES	4-WHEEL DISC
TOP SPEED	143MPH
ACCELERATION 0–60MPH	8.2 SECS
PRODUCTION SPAN	1984 →

Vorsprung Durch Technik **– ahead through technology is the Audi motto and the 200 Quattro is an excellent example of the company's advanced engineering and stylish packaging.**

F875 WNH

VW CORRADO

VW CORRADO

With the new Corrado, Volkswagen have taken the Scirocco concept into another stratosphere. Using the basic floorpan from the trend-setting Golf, the new Corrado will shake up the smaller sports coupé market. Looks apart, the Corrado is imbued with the GTi spirit but on a higher level.

Under the tight little bonnet lurks the Golf-derived 1,800cc 16-valve jewel which has made the GTi the benchmark of the world. Now, upped in output to 136bhp at 6,300rpm, the fuel-injected engine sprints the three-door-bodied car to 60mph in 8.7 seconds. But the Corrado isn't just a car to drive by throttle. Clever German engineering gives the back end passive rear-wheel steering, beating the Japanese at their own game with a far-simpler approach.

Cornering forces wrench the beam axle against track adjusting wedge-shaped bearings which promotes a neutral cornering line under hard driving. The front suspension is taken from the Golf GTi.

Sideways-on it's a baby Quattro, although from the front the Corrado could be a small Sierra. Looks aren't everything, and to prove the point – if 130mph wasn't sufficient indication that this is a rapid coupé to blow away the cobwebs – then the rock-steady handling, firm poise and superb cornering ability, coupled with such delicate touches as automatic spoilers and a slippery aerodynamic body (Cd 0.32) scream performance from every angle.

Depressingly, the car's designers spent so long under the bonnet and around the suspension mounts, they forgot to give the interior any sparkle at all. You could be sitting in a 'cooking' Golf judging by the cut of the cloth trim.

The drab furnishings, supportive yet unremarkable seats and overall mass produced-look cabin could have benefited from a few dabs of luxury to convince prospective buyers that this is a car-in-a-thousand, and keep them away from the Japanese opposition.

Perched on cast alloy 15in rims and running on Continental Super Contact 185/55 VR15s the Corrado hands down great traction at all speeds. Criticisms levelled at a harsh low speed ride vanish as the speedo swings upwards, and Porsche 944 owners start to look behind them, as pound-for-pound, their steeds start to lose ground. Overall the Corrado isn't as much of a Porsche-beater as VW might like, but in the medium coupé market the alarm bells should be ringing.

Volkswagen's new Corrado builds on a company tradition of small coupés that began in 1954 with the pretty Karmann-Ghia. The new car is *also* built by coachbuilder Karmann, but it's considerably quicker than its 1950s relative, particularly in supercharged form.

SPECIFICATION	
MODEL/TYPE	VOLKSWAGEN CORRADO 16V
ENGINE	4-Cyl, 1,781CC, DOHC
HORSEPOWER	136BHP @ 6,300RPM
TRANSMISSION	5-SPEED MANUAL
CHASSIS	STEEL MONOCOQUE
BRAKES	4-WHEEL DISC
TOP SPEED	131MPH
ACCELERATION 0–60MPH	8.7 SECS
PRODUCTION SPAN	1989 →

ITALY

Italy has long been the home of several famous makers of fast cars, albeit in small numbers, as befits any hand-made product. The very names of these manufacturers, Ferrari, Lancia, Maserati, Lamborghini, Alfa Romeo, even Fiat, conjure up an image of speed and high performance. The new name of Cizeta Moroder can be added to this list, in view of the newly-announced V16T.

I might reasonably begin this look at Italy by considering Lancia, a company older than all but Fiat of this group of makes and with a proud heritage of building and racing fast cars. In the last 20 years Lancia have suffered badly in the market place, despite enormous financial help from their current owners, the Fiat company. The Lancia has been an engineer's car, and their designers and chief engineers have been household names among Lancia owners. Vincenzo Lancia himself took an enormous pride in his company's products, and right up to his death in 1937, at the early age of 56, he would insist on evaluating on the road every single Lancia model, be it a prototype, research or pre-production car. If it did not at first meet his own very critical standards, the car simply didn't go on to the next stage in its development.

Although a fine racer himself in his early days, Vincenzo believed that sheer horsepower alone was not the way to make a fast car for a customer. Balance was the most immediate obvious feature in all Lancias that were built in Vincenzo's day. Although with the passage of time this characteristic was allowed to become less important, especially after the Fiat takeover, up to the end of the Vincenzo Lancia period all the Turin cars offered the best possible balance between roadholding and horsepower. Chassis performance was essential to the Lancia way of doing things.

It was always possible to find engines with more power per cc than a Lancia from other Italian makers, in particular from Alfa Romeo, and as most people are more instantly impressed by horsepower than by road abilities, Lancias began to appear as less than appealing cars. However, since the end of World War II Lancia models have emerged that must be considered real high performers by any standards.

They include cars like the B20 GT, one of the very first mass production cars properly to qualify for the title of Gran Turismo (and to my mind one of the most beautifully shaped cars of all time). It was also a car with a very honourable record in GT-class racing, scoring a second place in the Mille Miglia in 1951, winning the 1952 Targa Florio, the 1953 Liège–Rome–Liège, the 1954 Monte Carlo Rally and, as late as 1958, winning the Acropolis Rally. Then came the under-financed D50 Grand Prix racing car, which, with more financial backing might have seriously challenged the W196 Mercedes-Benz racing record. Various factory and Zagato-bodied Appias, Fulvias and Flaminias followed.

ALFA-ROMEO

ALFA ROMEO 164

The Alfa Romeo 164 is Alfa's first attempt at a large executive saloon since the Fiat take-over. Launched in 1988 in the UK, the V6 3-litre has been acclaimed as one of the sweetest large engines in production, and is endowed with a glorious exhaust note, so beloved of Alfa enthusiasts.

Driving through either a five-speed manual or four-speed automatic gearbox, the 164 is let down by dramatic torque-steer under hard acceleration. This is due to the front engine/front-drive layout, placing most weight over the front wheels. The engine is one of the largest front-drive units in production.

The 192bhp powerplant is mounted longitudinally in the Pininfarina-designed shell. On the move, the 164 demonstrates crisp, responsive acceleration, the car leaping through the gears readily under the urgent command of the driver's right foot. Cruising speeds convey little noise to the car's occupants, and the 164 gives a firm ride and safe, predictable handling.

There are two trim options, standard and Lusso, the latter shod with pretty 15in alloy wheels with Pirelli P4000 205/55 VR covers which grip with confidence, and allow spirited cornering. While the steering is power assisted, the system allows the driver plenty of feel, especially when it comes to transmission torque-steer characteristics at take-off. The 164 is a true high speed mile-eater, with fairly frugal tastes too, sipping one gallon every 24 miles on average. Despite having long overall gearing the power of the 3-litre allows the 164 to keep up with faster-geared competition.

The only area of the car to come in for severe criticism is the interior. Alfas have never been known for clear, easy-to-read instrumentation, and while the 164 breaks no new ground, some serious re-evaluation wouldn't come amiss back on the drawing board.

The Lusso version boasts a CD player as standard, though in line with the other controls, it's fiddly to use. Other modern comforts include air conditioning, electric seats, windows and mirrors.

Chiselling hard to erode the rusty reputation from the proud Alfa shield has partly been achieved by scrupulous protection of cars of the late 1980s, and this theme continues in the 164 with the galvanising of over 60% of the body.

Selling from £18,000 the 164 offers a lot of performance for the price. It's not a supercar, there are other 164 versions around to do the record-breaking, but rather the 164 saloon is a refined yet exciting car to own and drive.

The Alfa Romeo 164 looks similar to the Lancia Thema and Saab 9000 for a reason – all the cars share an identical platform. The 164 is gaining many new sales for Alfa Romeo, and there's even an automatic in the range (below). The 164 Procar prototype (right), although sharing the silhouette of the standard saloon, was a V10-powered racer that anticipated a race series which never actually happened.

S P E C I F I	C A T I O N
MODEL/TYPE	ALFA ROMEO 164
ENGINE	V6, 2,959CC
HORSEPOWER	192BHP @ 5,600RPM
TRANSMISSION	5-SPEED/4-SPEED AUTO
CHASSIS	STEEL MONOCOQUE
BRAKES	4-WHEEL DISC
TOP SPEED	138MPH
ACCELERATION 0–60MPH	7.9 SECS
PRODUCTION SPAN	1988 →

ALFA-ROMEO

ALFA ROMEO ES30

Alfa Romeo's links with Italian coachbuilder Zagato go back a long, long way — right back, in fact, to the 1920s, when Alfa's brilliant 1750 and 2300 chassis were clothed, as standard, with Zagato's pretty, functional spider bodywork.

It's gratifying, then, that Zagato is giving a helping hand in the renaissance of Alfa Romeo. Fiat, itself Italy's largest company, bought Alfa Romeo a few years ago and in a drive to revitalize the illustrious company's image, gave the go-ahead for a new, limited production coupé to be built on the basis of the traditional, rear-drive Alfa Romeo 75 saloon. Who else but Zagato, creator of such all-time greats as the Aston Martin DB4GTZ, Alfa Junior Z and countless special versions of Alfa's sporting models, to build it? The result is the ES30 coupé you see here.

Sitting on a shortened Alfa platform, with the rear-driven De Dion transaxle of that car — the clutch and gearbox sited together at the rear to give excellent weight distribution — the ES30 is ugly to some eyes, but chunky and purposeful to those who know what a thorough driver's car it is. Alfa claim that the ES30 is the first road car to truly capitalise on 'ground effect' aerodynamics, and the drag co-efficient of just 0.30 is exceptional for a car of just four metres in length.

The body is to be constructed from glass-reinforced plastic together with other plastic materials to form a composite structure and is reckoned to be extremely rigid. The car was designed principally in Alfa Romeo's own studios with some input from Zagato, in just 19 months. Zagato's coachbuliding division will construct the limited production run of 1000 cars, expected to sell like the proverbial hot cakes; the British allocation is believed, at the time of writing, to have been already virtually all snapped up.

Nought to 62mph, due to the car's low weight and brilliant ground adhesion, should be reached in a mere 7 seconds, and a top speed of well over 145mph is envisaged.

Alfa Romeo's new coupé, whatever its performance, will still have a distinctive and agressive look and will make a real change from the clinical nature of many so-called fast cars.

Alfa Romeo's fantastic new SZ coupé promises shattering performance and roadholding in a strictly limited edition of just 1000 cars; some have called it ugly, but 'not bland' would be a better description of its unusual lines.

S P E C I F I C A T I O N	
MODEL/TYPE	**ALFA ROMEO ES30**
ENGINE	**V6, 2,959CC, SOHC**
HORSEPOWER	**210BHP @ 6,200RPM**
TRANSMISSION	**5-SPEED MANUAL**
CHASSIS	**COMPOSITE MONOCOQUE**
BRAKES	**4-WHEEL DISC**
TOP SPEED	**145MPH**
ACCELERATION 0–60MPH	**7 SECS**
PRODUCTION SPAN	**1989 →**

FERRARI

Like the Porsche, Ferrari's cars are all capable of more than 125mph and several of them will beat this arbitrary figure by a very large margin. The two most recent, and to date fastest, Ferraris are the Testarossa and the GTO. Both names recall great Ferrari cars from the recent past and Ferrari have used them appropriately enough again on two machines that incorporate all the latest in high performance technology.

Ever since 1950, when Ferrari properly started to make and supply customer cars, as opposed to purely competition machinery, they have given pride of place to their engines. In the vast majority of cases these beautifully crafted power units have followed the overhead-cam V12 layout and plainly show the great influence that Enzo Ferrari himself has on the design philosophy of his company, even though he is now well into his 80s and the customer side of the business is owned by Fiat. As an ex-racer and racing team manager, his thirst for engine performance dominates his thinking on the Ferrari customer cars. It is not, however, quite as overwhelming as in the past, when the quality of design and performance of a Ferrari road-car engine was streets ahead of the rest of the car, which could often be described as no more than ordinary.

With the coming of 'science' into the closed shop of racing car design nearly 30 years ago, with Lotus's late founding-genius Colin Chapman in the forefront, Ferrari have been forced to take more heed of the other dynamic aspects of their racing cars. As with so many developments at Maranello, these have filtered down to keep their road cars in the vanguard of high performance vehicles. For the record, Ferrari probably make more of the components of their own cars than any other car maker in the world.

By Ferrari standards, the styling of the new Testarossa is wildly extravagant but, as ever, the real story lies under the skin—in this case centering on the 5-litre 'boxer' engine with its red crackle-finish cam covers that give the car its name, Red Head.

Ferrari

FERRARI

FERRARI GTO

Ferrari make no bones about the new GTO and describe it in their own literature as 'The Fastest Ferrari road car ever Built'. The GTO, which stands for *Gran Turismo Omologato,* is powered by a 2,855cc 32-valve V8 engine with twin turbochargers and developing a massive 400bhp at a typically Ferrari engine speed of 7,000rpm. The turbo system and its ancillaries use much of the technology developed on Ferrari's turbocharged Grand Prix cars. For instance, Weber-Marelli IAW electronic injection and ignition are used, with each bank of cylinders having its own separate system.The transmission is entirely designed and made by Ferrari, and the single composite unit comprises the five-speed gearbox, clutch and limited-slip differential.

Four-wheel ventilated disc brakes are fitted but ABS is not deemed necessary. Suspension follows the Grand Prix car

The Ferrari GTO, introduced in mid-1984, amply underlines Ferrari's continued commitment to ultimate performance—having finally overtaken the legendary front-engined V12 Daytona as the fastest ever Ferrari road car.

layout, being independent all round and with coil springs and Koni dampers providing the springing medium. Slightly different wheel sizes are employed at front and rear, being 16 × 8in front and 16 × 10in at the rear, while Goodyear NCT tyres are supplied as standard fittings.

The body styling is very similar, but not identical, to the 308GTB Ferrari, and extensive use was made of wind tunnel testing to achieve a very aerodynamic shape. To meet racing homologation requirements, as its name implies, only 200 GTOs were made and the prices were very high, at well over £75,000 in Britain for example.

On the performance front, the 'off-the-shelf' GTO is reckoned to be good for 189mph and acceleration is equally stunning, with 0–62mph possible in under 5 seconds. As it is obvious that the standard 400bhp can easily be uprated to as much as 600bhp, even more shattering performance can be anticipated from the competition versions which are this car's *raison d'etre*.

SPECIFICATION	
MODEL/TYPE	**FERRARI GTO**
ENGINE	**V8, 2,855CC, TURBO**
HORSEPOWER	**400BHP @ 7,000RPM**
TRANSMISSION	**5-SPEED MANUAL**
CHASSIS	**STEEL TUBULAR**
BRAKES	**4-WHEEL DISC**
TOP SPEED	**190MPH PLUS**
ACCELERATION 0–60MPH	**4.9 SECS**
PRODUCTION SPAN	**1985 ONLY**

FERRARI

FERRARI TESTAROSSA

The next Ferrari carries the name of one of the most beautiful competition cars ever to race, the Testarossa, or Red Head. This name was given to the car because its cam covers were painted red instead of the more usual black. In the year of the original car's introduction, 1958, it won the 1,000km of Buenos Aires, the Sebring 12 hours, the Targa Florio and Le Mans. During the next year, success followed success for this lovely looking machine and so it is no surprise that Ferrari have seen fit to restore the name to their latest high performance car in 1985. The power comes from a 4,942cc flat-12, four-valve-per-cylinder engine mounted amidships in the car, and on top of the transmission. This impressive powerhouse produces 390bhp at 6,300rpm, to give the 1985 Testarossa a top speed of 181mph and acceleration from 0 to 62mph in 5.8 seconds.

The stunning body, like its predecessor, is from the studios of Pininfarina and, also like the earlier car, is like nothing else around today. The new radiator position, in the middle of the car instead of in the more usual place at the front, has been accommodated successfully in the body styling and although the car has its critics, to my mind Pininfarina have done an excellent job.

The Testarossa's interior continues the constant improvement in driver and passenger accommodation that Ferraris have shown in the last few years and at the speeds that this car is capable of only the best ergonomics could be deemed as right. Noted journalist and former Ferrari team driver, Paul Frére, testing the new Testarossa, commented on the excellent roadholding and ride, the steering and braking performance, but added that the Ferrari trait of placing more emphasis on the engine than the chassis still remains in this latest Ferrari. Much as things change, they still remain the same, especially at Maranello!

The incredible looks of the Ferrari Testarossa, as well as its amazing performance, have already made the car a legend in its own lifetime, and an object of desire for every red-blooded fast car fan.

SPECIFICATION	
MODEL/TYPE	FERRARI TESTAROSSA
ENGINE	FLAT 12-CYL, DOHC
HORSEPOWER	390BHP @ 6,300RPM
TRANSMISSION	5-SPEED MANUAL
CHASSIS	TUBULAR STEEL
BRAKES	4-WHEEL DISC
TOP SPEED	181MPH
ACCELERATION 0–62MPH	5.8 SECS
PRODUCTION SPAN	1985 →

FERRARI

FERRARI 348

The 328 is dead, long live the 348! To say that the 328's successor was overdue would be to slight a magnificent sports car, but as we move into the 1990s, a fresh image emerges. The 348 uses a quad-cam V8 to achieve over 300bhp, and vague references to both Testarossa and 328 have been made in the new car's styling.

The 348 is wider, with a broad, grinning front grille, no longer hiding the radiator – for that has moved rearwards to join the engine.

The V8 is mounted low down, longitudinally, enhancing the low centre of gravity. Opening up the 3405cc motor reveals 300bhp at 7,200rpm, fuel being precisely metered through the latest Motronic fuel injection system. The 348's is a tractable engine. Slip the clutch at 1,000rpm and the car lumbers away, floor the throttle and the exhausts scream with joy, and the invariably red, squat, two-seaters screech away. If you're neglectful, the rev limiter cuts in at 7,800rpm, a gentle reminder that there are other cogs to choose, and should you find an open enough stretch, over 170mph is, theoretically, possible.

Handling is to usual Ferrari standards, giving precise dynamic feedback from the wide 255/45ZR17 tyres and direct steering; there's no power assistance on this model. Handling is sharp, predictable and there's barely a vague inference of body roll. If you drive recklessly the back end will try to lead the nose, but no serious Ferrari driver should ever experience that.

Inside the car there's plenty of room, though not much space for storage. Driver's seat is low and the wide, sweeping screen only shows a small part of the long nose. Perhaps the only area where the 348 can be criticised is its weight. The 348tb weighs in at 3,065lbs, but with such a well-tuned and developed 3.4-litre V8 the weight penalty shouldn't be too great.

SPECIFICATION	
MODEL/TYPE	FERRARI 348
ENGINE	V8, 3,405CC, QUAD CAM
HORSEPOWER	300BHP @ 7,200RPM
TRANSMISSION	5-SPEED MANUAL
CHASSIS	STEEL TUBULAR
BRAKES	4-WHEEL DISC
TOP SPEED	171MPH
ACCELERATION 0–60MPH	5.6 SECS
PRODUCTION SPAN	1989 →

FERRARI

FERRARI 412

Pininfarina's 412 2+2 coupé body has that rare gift of timeless elegance. After so many years the lines still look crisp and up to date. Under that marvellous sleek bonnet lies a V12, bored out to 4,942cc, which can effortlessly sweep the car's occupants to 60mph in 8.3 seconds, and on to a top speed of 155mph. A three-speed automatic transmission is standard but a five-speed manual is also available.

This Ferrari is a full four-seater, the rear passengers haven't been forgotten by the designers, making the car a fast comfortable cruiser.

In true Ferrari tradition, the 412, last of the front-engined V12s, performs magnificently. It's a refined tourer as opposed to an out-and-out racer, for the Ferrari owner who has grown beyond traffic light sprinting starts. But the 412 isn't only a long-distance tourer; it has the air of an opulent town car, while maintaining a high degree of understatement. The 412 doesn't prance on its hind legs and bellow that it's a blood red Ferrari out to eat all competition. No, this is a gentleman's carriage.

Until the arrival of the BMW V12 in 1987, the Ferrari 412 and Jaguar V12 were the only V12 engines Europe produced.

Inside the 412's cabin a high level of trim is specified, sumptuous leather upholstery, electrically-operated door windows, air conditioning, central door locking and electric mirrors. The dash and centre console look chunky and square in comparison with the sleek body lines. That apart, the car is extremely well put together and a joy to drive. Sitting close to the ground the 412 owes much to its supercar brethren. Squat, low-profile 240/55VR16 Goodyears stick close to the tarmac and handling provided by this high performance rubber is faultless.

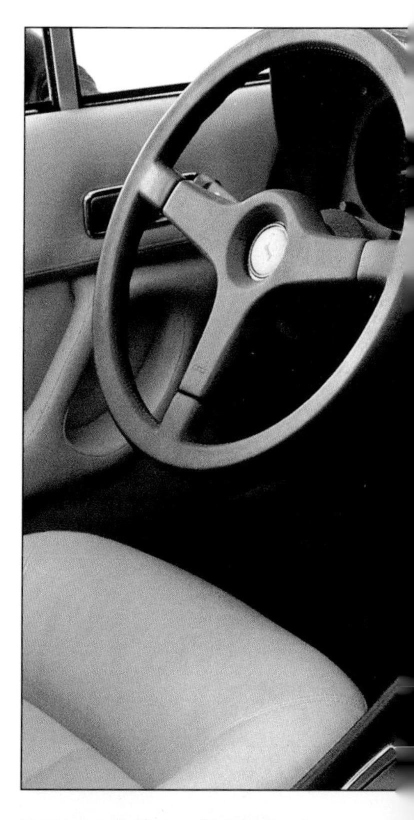

For years (in its various guises) the Ferrari 412 was the only V12 four-seater GT alternative to the Jaguar XJS. With new V12 sportsters coming from BMW and Mercedes, the competition is likely to get stronger, but the 'old money' chic of this Ferrari four-seater seems to ensure it a little more life yet.

SPECIFICATION	
MODEL/TYPE	FERRARI 412
ENGINE	V12, 4,942CC, QUAD CAM
HORSEPOWER	340BHP @ 6,000RPM
TRANSMISSION	3-SP AUTO/5-MANUAL
CHASSIS	TUBULAR STEEL
BRAKES	4-WHEEL DISC
TOP SPEED	155.3MPH
ACCELERATION 0–60MPH	8.3 SECS
PRODUCTION SPAN	1982 →

pininfarina

FERRARI

FERRARI F40

Under the Kevlar and composite skin of the Ferrari F40 lies a V8 capable of slinging the hotshot supercar to 124mph in 12 secs. Built on the express orders of the late Enzo Ferrari, the F40 commemorates the 40th anniversary of the firm and is a reminder of the great days at Le Mans and all that is wonderful about Ferrari. Taking much of the design brief direct from the racing cars of the day, the F40 team clothed a sweet tubular steel chassis in the most advanced fabrics yet. The result is a car which stops people in their tracks on looks alone, and silences competition with one stiff prod of the accelerator pedal. The F40 is a *very* fast car: over 478bhp from 2,936cc, via two turbochargers, four cams and four valves per cylinder.

Under the see-through Plexiglass engine cover which also makes up the rear window, the 3-litre V8 sits, bared for all to see. The wide but not very deep bonnet precedes a steeply-raked screen and wide front wings cover Pirelli P700s fitted to 8×17 rims.

The highly noticeable rear wing was a late design addition, but works well to keep the rear 13×17 rims, covered by 335/35ZR 17, stuck on to the tarmac at speeds approaching 200mph.

Getting behind the wheel itself is a contortionist's delight, but once entrenched in the tight-fitting bucket seat, full race harness clipped up, the twist of the ignition key brings all eight howling cylinders to life. Plant the accelerator into the floor and you're off; change up at 7,000 rpm, through the gearbox and you're travelling really fast by the time you reach fourth. The wail behind the driver's head gives the impression that a battallion of frenzied banshees have been let loose, and it's important to keep concentrating on the road – and the car.

The F40 handles like any pure race car should, firmly and with confidence. If softer driving styles are preferred, ride height and shock absorber settings can be adjusted from the driver's seat.

The F40 is low, rakish, has carefully set-up suspension and wildly-tuned engine, a true all-out performer and egotistical heaven for both company and driver. And so it should be, considering the 40 years development work that's gone into it. Priced at around £140,000 when put on sale originally, in the 1990s any examples selling below half a million pounds will be absolute bargains.

This car – the Ferrari F40 – is the object of desire for virtually every red-blooded sports car enthusiast of the 1990s. Not only is it shatteringly fast but it's also stunningly outrageous in its styling, and never has a single pound, dollar or yen been lost in an F40 purchase.

SPECIFICATION	
MODEL/TYPE	**FERRARI F40**
ENGINE	**V8, 2,936CC, QUAD CAM**
HORSEPOWER	**478BHP @ 7,750RPM**
TRANSMISSION	**5-SPEED MANUAL**
CHASSIS	**STEEL TUBULAR CHASSIS/ COMPOSITE BODY**
BRAKES	**4-WHEEL DISC**
TOP SPEED	**201MPH**
ACCELERATION 0–60MPH	**4 SECS**
PRODUCTION SPAN	**1987 →**

MASERATI

MASERATI BITURBO

SPECIFICATION	
MODEL/TYPE	MASERATI BITURBO SPYDER
ENGINE	V6, 2,790CC
HORSEPOWER	225BHP @ 5,500RPM
TRANSMISSION	5-SP MANUAL/4-SP AUTO
CHASSIS	STEEL MONOCOQUE
BRAKES	4-WHEEL DISC
TOP SPEED	150MPH
ACCELERATION 0–60MPH	6 SECS
PRODUCTION SPAN	1985 →

Maserati's great Biturbo coupé looks even better without its tin roof. Bringing new elegance to fast luxurious travelling, the Spyder performs just as well as its forebears, in true Maserati style. The twin turbos help to extract 225bhp from the 2.8-litre V6. Although it might ruffle your hair, getting to 60mph will take less than six seconds, and top end speed is quoted at 150mph.

The Spyder is finished to the usual high Maserati standards: wood inlays, sumptuous seats, a full complement of accessories, and a rather incongruous analogue timepiece sited in the centre of the dashboard.

Under the bonnet there lies a complex electronic fuel and ignition system, which monitors and regulates the engine ensuring that there is no damaging overboosting, pre-ignition or over-revving.

Although the bodystyle has been around for a while now, Maserati have managed clever and regular updating to keep the appearance crisp and appealing to the eye.

The driving experience has not diminished through time; the Spyder is more than capable of giving other prestige drophead manufacturers a run for their money.

MASERATI

MASERATI MERAK SS

The Merak was first shown at the 1972 Geneva Motor Show. As with all Giugiaro-styled cars, it is very good looking, from every angle. Fit and finish of the bodywork are good rather than excellent and like all Italian cars, whatever their cost, any lapse in maintenance, cosmetic or mechanical, very soon shows itself. Some neglected five-year-old Meraks look ten times their age, while equally old models that have received regular loving attention look almost new.

Any mid-engined 2+2 car loses out in two major respects over more conventional, front-engined models, in accessibility to the engine and in a definite lack of real luggage carrying capacity. In these failings, however, the Merak is no better or worse than any similar car, and in one other respect the Merak is outstandingly good for a mid-engined car; unlike most, its three-quarter rear view vision is good, as the usual blind spot is much reduced by the use of the flying buttress rear window arrangement devised by Giugiaro.

The Merak SS's engine is a 2,965cc V6 with double overhead camshafts driven by a duplex chain. This engine produces 208bhp at 5,800rpm on three Weber twin-choke carburettors — two are 42DCNF31s and the third is a single 42DCNF32. This is enough to carry the car to a top speed of 143mph. However, there is one drawback to this engine, on driving the Merak at maximum revs for any length of time an alarming drop in registered oil pressure is noticed. This may be due to the all-alloy engine flexing, allowing the main bearings to release pressure, with dire effects on engine life. The maker's handbook simply recommends that the engine shouldn't be run at maximum speed for extended periods but there is no rev-limiting device to guard against this problem.

The lack of a modern fuel-injection system shows up in temperamental cold starts and fussy driving habits until the engine is fully warmed up. Fuel consumption averages out at about 18mpg, so that even with the 18.7-gallon tank only about 350 miles are possible between refills.

On the road, the Merak behaves like any good mid-engined car. It is stable, with a reasonable amount of understeer at all times, its ride is choppy at low speeds, improving with an increase in speed to become acceptable. Braking is by the Citroën high-pressure system and really isn't well suited to such a high performance machine, as its over-sensitivity hardly makes for smooth, fast progress.

The driving compartment is comfortable, with enough room for two average-sized adults, but the heating and ventilation systems are no better than poor, taking a very long time to warm up and then control of the heat is difficult and the ventilation almost non-existent! Air-conditioning was available as an extra, really a necessity. The Merak was not a cheap car and was for Maserati lovers only as there were certainly better value cars of similar performance on the market.

Somehow, the Maserati name has never had quite the same cachet as Ferrari, but the Neptune's trident badge of the city of Bologna has nonetheless graced some superb cars.
The Maserati Merak SS (opposite and previous page) was introduced in 1975, the year in which Citroën, who had rescued the Bolognese company in 1968, relinquished control to Alessandro de Tomaso, Under de Tomaso's management, Maserati has made a remarkable recovery and for once in its troubled history can face the future with real confidence.

S P E C I F I C A T I O N	
MODEL/TYPE	**MASERATI MERAK SS**
ENGINE	**V6, 2,965CC SOHC**
HORSEPOWER	**208BHP @ 5,800RPM**
TRANSMISSION	**5-SPEED MANUAL**
CHASSIS	**STEEL MONOCOQUE**
BRAKES	**4-WHEEL DISC**
TOP SPEED	**143MPH**
ACCELERATION 0–60MPH	**7.7 SECS**
PRODUCTION SPAN	1972–83

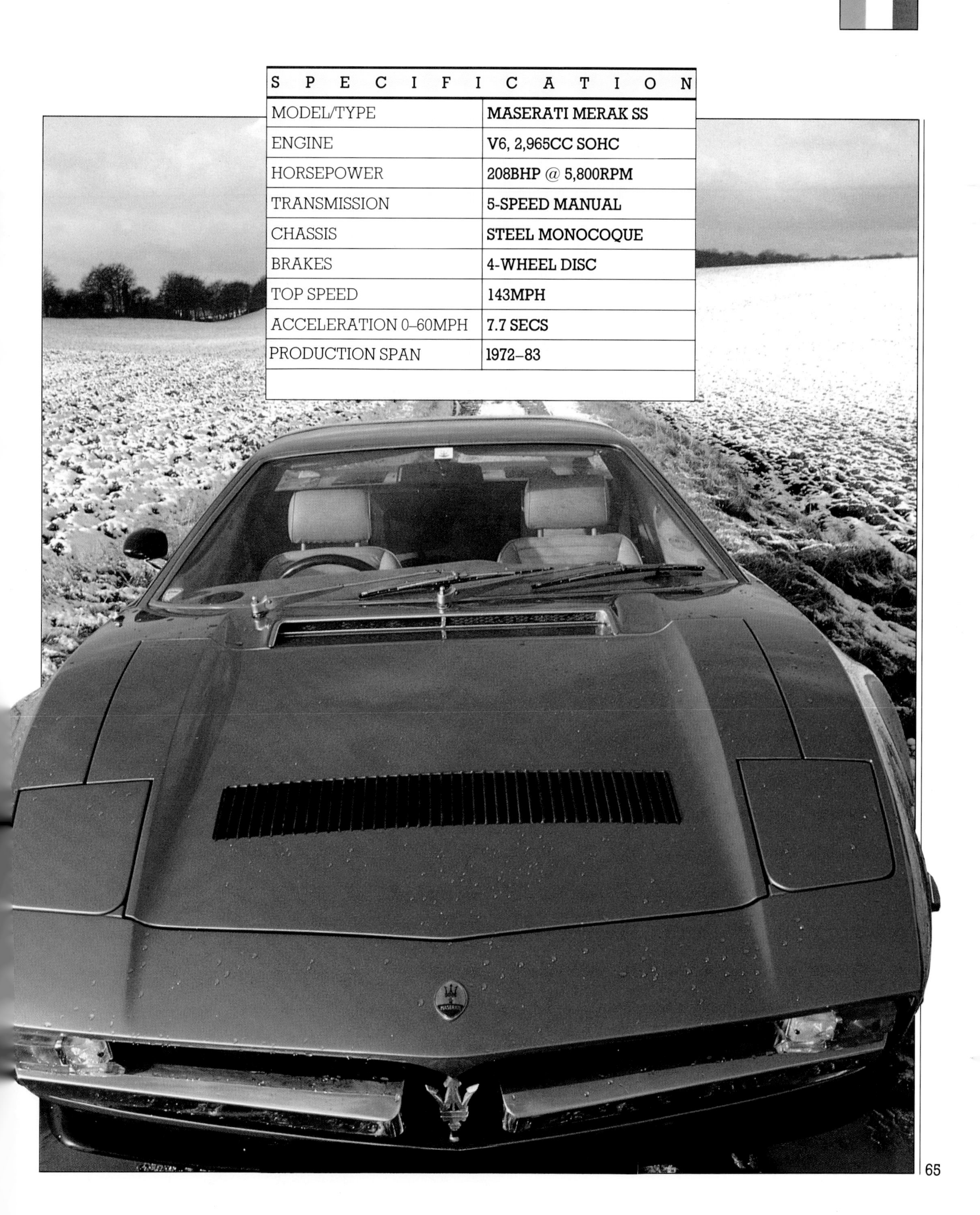

MASERATI

MASERATI KHAMSIN

The Khamsin model is the final embodiment of the great front-engined, high-speed Maseratis, like the Mexico and the Mistral. As a design it is now nearly 20 years old and many aspects of the car show this fact very clearly. The handsome body houses a front-mounted 4,700cc V8 engine, with double overhead cams, driven by a duplex chain. This power unit breathes through four Weber 42DCNF41 carburettors and produces 280bhp at 5,500rpm.

The Khamsin body although officially described as a 2+2 is really only a two-seater, as rear leg and head room are minimal at best. Accommodation for two, however, is comfortable, although the seats are covered in rather slippery leather, which, together with a strange lack of lateral support makes for less than positive driver location. The steering and seats are adjusted hydraulically, and the steering column can be adjusted for both length and rake by this system. The body styling is tasteful and the car is very well finished. The Khamsin was also reasonably priced for a car that would reach 160mph and accelerate from 0 to 60mph in 6.5 seconds.

S P E C I F I C A T I O N	
MODEL/TYPE	MASERATI KHAMSIN
ENGINE	V8, 4,700CC DOHC
HORSEPOWER	280BHP @ 5,500RPM
TRANSMISSION	5-SPEED MANUAL
CHASSIS	STEEL MONOCOQUE
BRAKES	4-WHEEL DISC
TOP SPEED	160MPH
ACCELERATION 0–60MPH	6.5 SECS
PRODUCTION SPAN	1973–82

Although the Bertone-styled Maserati Khamsin, introduced in 1974, is now growing somewhat long in the tooth, it must still be regarded as a classic example of the traditional big front-engined supercar.

LAMBORGHINI

LAMBORGHINI COUNTACH

Lamborghini is a relative newcomer among the classic Italian makes, but its engineering is second to none. The Countach Anniversary is the final farewell to a striking design which is now almost 20 years old. Styling is outrageously extrovert and dramatic – even standing still the car looks like it's moving at over 100mph. When you *do* slip behind the wheel, after lifting the gullwing door, the sparkling V12 5-litre will launch you into another orbit.

Sixty miles per hour approaches after a scant five seconds and the car accelerates all the way to 183mph given a straight enough stretch of open road.

The Anniversary special is the last of the line, the final refinement of Gandini's masterpiece. Powered by the uprated V12 now pumping out 445bhp at 7,000rpm the car's performance more than adequately lives up to its appearance. Creating a stir wherever you turn up and attracting lots of police attention are two omni-present reactions to Countach ownership. However, it's a motoring legend practically unmatched in its lifetime, or probably beyond.

While round town driving might prove frustrating, the Countach comes into its own on fast roads, and it's not afraid of a few bends either. Fat 225/50 VR15 tyres on the front and 345/35VR15 at the rear endow the car with superior grip, cornering at highly illegal speeds is achieved without fuss or drama in the right hands. Stopping the car presents no problems, with over 1.1g deceleration provided by ventilated front and rear discs. Drivers will be surprised if they ever see fuel consumption much over 20 mpg, but who buys a car like this to worry about the petrol bills? Priced at close on £100,000 it isn't only the car's performance and looks which are out of this world.

If you've got it flaunt it! The unashamedly striking lines of the Countach Anniversary are to be savoured. Only 430 left to be built and then it's the end of the line.

SPECIFICATION	
MODEL/TYPE	LAMBORGHINI COUNTACH ANNIVERSARY
ENGINE	V12, 5,167CC, DOHC
HORSEPOWER	445BHP @ 7,000RPM
TRANSMISSION	5-SPEED MANUAL
CHASSIS	STEEL MONOCOQUE
BRAKES	4-WHEEL DISC
TOP SPEED	183MPH
ACCELERATION 0–60MPH	5.0 SECS
PRODUCTION SPAN	1989 →

GREAT BRITAIN

Great Britain has always had its share of the fast car market, from Napiers before World War I, Bentleys after it, and Jaguars, Aston Martins, Bristols and AC Cobras since. Unlike those of many other countries, the British fast car industry has been heavily handicapped by speed limits, high insurance premiums and by the lack of a really rich mass of population wanting, and able to buy, expensive fast cars. However, in today's world and in spite of speed limits, there are more fast cars available to the British consumer than at any time in the country's motoring history. They range from the very expensive to the affordable. I will comment on thirteen (out of a list of several more) in this chapter.

The Virage is the car Aston Martin is pinning its hopes on in the 1990s but, while its competitors from Germany and Italy become ever more technically advanced, the graceful new Aston sticks faithfully to the old-fashioned cocktail of front engine, rear-wheel drive, hand-crafted aluminium bodywork, and hand-assembled V8 engine.

ASTON MARTIN VIRAGE

The new Aston Martin V8 to take the exclusive sports car manufacturer into the 1990s is the Virage. Following in the footsteps of the illustrious and much-developed V8 of the past two decades, the Virage has a hard act to follow.

Ken Greenley and John Hefferman, two of Britain's leading automotive designers, have come up with a more rounded and svelte looking coupé for the next decade. While the car looks smaller than the muscular V8, the Virage has plenty of performance tucked away under that flat bonnet. The new V8 comes with four-valves-per-cylinder, cast aluminium block, and two camshafts per bank. Bored out to 5,340cc, the Virage thumps its way to 60mph in a scant 6 seconds and top speed is well over 160mph.

The Virage was designed using the latest computer technology and indeed the entire car is more modern and up-to-date. The traditional wood and leather remain, as does the Aston charm, not to mention the initial selling price of just less than £100,000.

Sitting on pretty cast aluminium 16in wheels covered by Avon Turbospeeds (255/60ZR16s) the Virage looks hungry for speed. Whistle the car along a straight or winding road and you'll appreciate the hours of development miles put into the suspension set-up. The way the controls fall readily to hand and the purr of the contented V8 working away in front of you.

There can't be many supercars left that are this refined, still able to pull in such impressive performance figures and built with the convenience of front engine layout. While handling may suffer slightly from the front end bias, the weight distribution is such that only in extreme circumstances will the back end pop out. There's a refreshing lack of gimmicky electronics in the Virage too. Few Aston owners want specific immediate fuel consumption readout or need to know the time in Tokyo. Rather, Aston Martin Virage drivers feel cossetted by the knowledge that the hand-built V8 was put together by the world's finest engine builder, who took many days to complete such a work of art that he inscribed his name on a tag on the engine itself.

SPECIFICATION	
MODEL/TYPE	ASTON MARTIN VIRAGE
ENGINE	V8, 5,340CC, QUAD CAM
HORSEPOWER	330BHP @ 5,500RPM
TRANSMISSION	5-SPEED MANUAL/ 3-SP AUTO
CHASSIS	STEEL
BRAKES	4-WHEEL DISC
TOP SPEED	155MPH
ACCELERATION 0–60MPH	6 SECS
PRODUCTION SPAN	1990 →

ASTON MARTIN

ASTON MARTIN LAGONDA

The Lagonda has a 5,340cc double overhead cam V8 engine breathing through four Weber 42DCNF90/100 carburettors. The Aston Martin factory in the small town of Newport Pagnell does not quote horsepower figures but the German ministry of transport requires all cars sold in the Federal Republic to disclose their power outputs and for that requirement Aston Martin have quoted a figure of 390bhp, which must be close to the mark.

Transmission from the front-mounted engine is via a Chrysler Torqueflite automatic gearbox to a chassis-mounted limited-slip differential. Front suspension is by the classic unequal length wishbone, coil-spring and damper set up, with an anti-roll bar. The rear suspension is self-levelling and features a de Dion axle. Steering is by power-assisted rack and pinion and brakes are ventilated disc units all round. The Lagonda uses 15 × 6in alloy wheels fitted as standard with the superb Avon Turbospeed 235/70 VR 15 tyres.

The car's instruments use digital LED displays and cover all possible information that the driver may need. The Lagonda weighs 4,622lb, has a top speed of 143mph and takes just 20.8 seconds to reach 100mph from a standstill. The William Towns-designed body is striking in appearance and certainly has looks in keeping with the price. The whole car exudes luxury and high performance

This classic power unit was introduced in 1970 and by 1972 it had replaced the long-serving six-cylinder unit as the standard Aston Martin engine. Most specialist manufacturers looking for more horsepower tend to turn to big, easily available American V8s but it is typical of Aston Martin's integrity that they looked to their own drawing boards and came up with an engine which powers not only their road cars but also the company's Nimrod Group C racing sportscar.

SPECIFICATION	
MODEL/TYPE	ASTON MARTIN Lagonda
ENGINE	V8, 5,340CC, SOHC
HORSEPOWER	N/A
TRANSMISSION	3-SPEED AUTO
CHASSIS	STEEL
BRAKES	4-WHEEL DISC
TOP SPEED	143MPH
ACCELERATION 0–60MPH	8.9 SECS
PRODUCTION SPAN	1980 →

It's been around since 1976 and by 1986 was looking very dated, so the Lagonda was 'softened' with a new body style by its original stylist William Towns, to give it a few more years of life.

AML 1

ASTON MARTIN VANTAGE

The Aston Martin Vantage is a sports coupé in the old style, big, very fast, very expensive, constructed in the finest materials, and very beautifully finished. The car uses the same hand-built V8 engine as the Lagonda but with high-performance camshafts and bigger Weber 48IDF 3/150 carburettors increasing both power and torque. The gearbox is the ZF five-speed manual model which is heavy in operation but otherwise superb. Wheel sizes are also uprated compared to the Lagonda, to 15 × 8in and standard tyres are 275/55 VR 15 Pirelli P7s.

The Vantage is shatteringly fast, with a 168mph top speed and acceleration from 0 to 100mph in 11.9 seconds. Don't ask about fuel consumption which averages only 9–10mpg; in this league, such calculations never come into the equation. For such a large car, the Vantage is, surprisingly, really only a two-seater. Space for passengers in the back is, at best, minimal. Agility on twisty roads is obviously limited by sheer size, the car being much more suitable for long high-speed journeys preferably by unrestricted motorway.

The Aston Martin Vantage is the ultimate example of the traditional British sports coupé and if it is ever dropped from production by the powers-that-be at Newport Pagnell it will be sorely missed, even by those who will never be able to afford to buy one.

The Aston Martin Vantage (*inset*) and the drophead Volante (*below*) both look, and indeed feel, big, but their lusty V8 engines — all built by hand and each bearing its builder's name on a brass plate — make them two of the fastest cars in the world.

SPECIFICATION	
MODEL/TYPE	**ASTON MARTIN Vantage**
ENGINE	**V8, 5,340CC, SOHC**
HORSEPOWER	**N/A**
TRANSMISSION	**5-SPEED MANUAL**
CHASSIS	**STEEL**
BRAKES	**4-WHEEL DISC**
TOP SPEED	**168MPH**
ACCELERATION 0–60MPH	**5.2 SECS**
PRODUCTION SPAN	**1978 →**

BRISTOL

Next on the list are three cars from the Bristol Car Company, the Britannia, the Beaufighter and the Brigand—all named after famous Bristol aircraft from the company's earlier days. Although Bristol now use American V8 engines, the big, luxuriously appointed and extremely quick cars are in reality archetypally British. They are thoroughly conventional, even a little old fashioned in overall concept, but what they lack in high technology or advanced thinking they more than make up for in engineering quality.

This is a logical result of a background in aero engineering, where fundamental change is slow but quality is everything. Aircraft were Bristol's forté up to the end of the war in 1945, when the Bristol Aircraft Company sought new employment for suddenly redundant production capacity and opened a car division—which had been under consideration even during the war.

The first Bristol car, launched in 1947, was based on much-improved prewar BMW six-cylinder engines and chassis, rights to which Bristol had acquired as wartime reparations. Bristol's main improvements to the BMW engines were in the use of superior materials—unavailable in prewar Germany as high-grade metals were already being diverted to military use.

With these first cars, the Bristol reputation for performance with quality was born. The Bristol has never been a slavish follower of fashion, never for instance changing its shape simply to attract a fickle buying public. The cars are made by hand, slowly and at a rate of only three a week. They are bought and driven, usually with some verve, by real enthusiasts. Packard used to use the slogan 'Ask the man who owns one' and every Packard owner by implication became an unpaid salesman. Bristol might use the same words; every single Bristol owner I have ever met loves his car (or sometimes cars) and cannot wait to start selling the virtues of the make to anyone who will listen.

From the BMW-engined models, Bristol developed their own, classic, hemi-headed straight-six engine and this, in superbly developed chassis, was used until 1961. Then, having rejected the option of building their own V8 engine as being too expensive for three cars a week, Bristol began its association with American power which continues in the superb cars described here.

BRISTOL BRIGAND

The most expensive of the current Bristol range is the Brigand, a turobocharged two-door four-seater saloon whose sleek lines date back to 1976 and the introduction of what was then known as the 603 saloon. The Brigand costs a few pounds more than the throughbred Aston Martin Vantage and not much less than the normally-aspirated version of the Bentley Mulsanne – each of which uses its own design and make of V8. This is not

to imply that the Bristol is in any way inferior, in fact at least one magazine road-tester has described the Bristol as being, overall, the best car in the world, at any price.

That, as with any car, is open to endless argument, but with a top speed of 150mph and the ability to reach 60mph from rest in under six seconds, the Brigand is not as quick as the Vantage (but then nor is much else) but will comfortably out-run the 'ordinary' Mulsanne.

Part of the Bristol's strength lies in its chassis performance, where the engineering quality is really evident, and although it will give best place to many modern supercars, its ride and handling are quite exceptional for such a luxurious, spacious saloon.

SPECIFICATION	
MODEL/TYPE	BRISTOL BRIGAND
ENGINE	CHRYSLER V8, TURBO
HORSEPOWER	N/A
TRANSMISSION	CHRYSLER AUTO
CHASSIS	BOX SECTION STEEL
BRAKES	4-WHEEL DISC
TOP SPEED	150MPH
ACCELERATION 0–60MPH	5.9 SECS
PRODUCTION SPAN	1984 →

Although many other Anglo-American hybrids have been hastily conceived and appropriately short-lived, the 140mph Bristol Britannia saloon shows that a marriage of the best British engineering and an American mass-produced power unit can result in a genuine classic car.

BRISTOL

SPECIFICATION	
MODEL/TYPE	BRISTOL BEAUFIGHTER
ENGINE	CHRYSLER V8, TURBO
HORSEPOWER	N/A
TRANSMISSION	CHRYSLER AUTO
CHASSIS	STEEL BOX SECTION
BRAKES	4-WHEEL DISC
TOP SPEED	150MPH
ACCELERATION 0–60MPH	5.9 SECS
PRODUCTION SPAN	1984 →

BRISTOL BEAUFIGHTER

The most glamorous of the Bristol range, if such a term is appropriate, is the turbocharged Beaufighter, which shares the same version of the Chrysler hemi as the Brigand saloon. The Beaufighter however is a much more distinctive and rather angular car, distinguished by its flamboyant targa-type top, with a substantial roll-hoop and a lift off centre section.

The car was styled by Zagato and introduced as the 412 Convertible, later known as the Convertible Saloon, in 1975. Also among its styling features is the traditional Bristol way of housing the spare wheel in a concealed compartment in the front wing. The turbocharged version and the Beaufighter name were launched in 1980 and the superb car has been little changed since then.

Like the similarly-powered Brigand, it will reach 150mph and cover zero to 60mph in 5.9 seconds. The Beaufighter is the cheapest car in the Bristol range but it's still a costly automobile, on the British market it is marginally more expensive than the cheapest Aston Martin or the newly introduced Bentley Eight – its most obvious esoteric British rivals. Price however is not the most important consideration at this end of the market and the Bristol appeal is unique. For such large, heavy and well-equipped machines they are surprisingly light in feel, easy to drive well and only a little harder to drive really quickly. What more could any sybaritic enthusiast ask?

BENTLEY

BENTLEY MULSANNE

When the Bentley company was sold to Rolls-Royce in 1931 it was soon apparent that the old Bentley, the blood-and-guts fast sportscar, would be smoothed and softened into no more than a very nice but unremarkable open Rolls-Royce, and the days of real performance would be over. It took Rolls-Royce 51 years to introduce a Bentley that was more than a re-badged, re-radiatored Rolls-Royce. The Mulsanne model, named after the famous straight on the Le Mans racing circuit, the scene of the beginning of the old Bentley legend, is, at last, a really fast Bentley, one that W. O. Bentley himself would certainly not have disowned. W.O. always disliked and would have nothing to do with supercharged engines, feeling that if more power was required he could easily provide it with more capacity, while retaining all the flexibility and reliability that his cars were renowned for. In his day the supercharger was not for the ordinary motorist and was justifiably viewed with suspicion when fitted to an everyday car.

The Mulsanne has changed all that, for it is one of the very best of the current crop of boosted induction cars. Its 6.75-litre V8 engine produces an undisclosed amount of power, but sufficient to propel the heavy car (weighing 5,051lb) to speeds of over 130mph and from zero to 60mph in 7.4 seconds. It seats four people in great comfort and can transport them with a smoothness and speed that are uncanny. Handling is a little 'soft', with rather too much roll in cornering but a Bentley is not usually hustled around like a Ferrari and with normal Bentley-style driving it is a delight — albeit an expensive delight. Rolls-Royce-made automobiles have a justified reputation for retaining their resale value.

SPECIFICATION	
MODEL/TYPE	BENTLEY MULSANNE
ENGINE	V8, 6,750CC, TURBO
HORSEPOWER	N/A
TRANSMISSION	3-SPEED AUTO
CHASSIS	STEEL MONOCOQUE
BRAKES	4-WHEEL DISC
TOP SPEED	135MPH
ACCELERATION 0–60MPH	7.4 SECS
PRODUCTION SPAN	1982→

Ettore Bugatti once described the Bentleys which beat his own cars at Le Mans in the 1920s as *'les plus vites camions du monde'*—the fastest lorries in the world. No lorry however was ever as fast or as luxurious as the Bentley Mulsanne, named for the famous straight on the Le Mans circuit where Bentleys had their finest hour.

FORD

FORD SIERRA COSWORTH RS500

Since the incredibly successful Ford Capri was dropped from Ford's line-up in 1987, the manufacturer has not offered a replacement for its coupé, the car that was once dubbed 'the car you always promised yourself', and that had dominated sales of sporty coupés since its introduction in 1969.

Ford, however, has not given up on performance cars even if the dashing looks of the Capri have been firmly consigned to history — the Ford Sierra Cosworth RS500 you see here can exceed 150mph and has been winning battles on the race-tracks of Europe in the European Touring Car Championship . . . a race series for which the car was specifically devised. The RS500 was meant to be a racing car right from the beginning.

The blue oval has been closely involved with motor sport at most levels since the sixties, and Fords have been rally, race-track and Formula One champions. The ETC was one area where the company was strong but in order to continue its participation, a new version of the rear-wheel-drive Sierra RS Cosworth was called for. Therefore coachbuilding and engineering specialist Aston Martin Tickford was commissioned to build 500 'homologation special' RS500s in double-quick time — the whole batch was completed in just seven months, most destined for road car buyers.

The Sierra RS Cosworth is already a fast car, with its Cosworth-developed engine; this features twin-overhead camshafts, four valves per cylinder with the head cast in aluminium alloy, Weber-Marelli multi-point fuel-injection, and a Garrett AiResearch T3 turbocharger. Power is 204bhp at 6000rpm, with maximum torque of 205lb ft at 4500rpm.

With a larger turbo and intercooler, changes to fuel-injection and cooling system, a strengthened engine block to withstand the 400bhp that the racing versions would put out, the power available on the RS500 was upped to 224bhp. The car also comes with anti-lock brakes and a close-ratio Borg Warner five-speed gearbox.

These modifications mean that the car, as tested by *Autocar* magazine, can genuinely better 150mph, giving a mean maximum of 154 — not bad going for a car with a 2-litre four-cylinder basic engine. It's maybe not as tractable as the old Ford Capri, particularly the Tickford-modified and turbo-charged version, with its coil-sprung, trailing arm rear suspension instead of the Capri's old 'live' axle, but the RS500 won the championship convincingly. All the cars made, of course, were sold instantly.

At the other end of the price and exclusivity spectrum are Ford's two fast cars in Great Britain, the XR4×4 and the RS 500 Cosworth Sierra. These two follow in the tradition of all Ford products in offering fine value-for-money vehicles, and in both cases they also have the bonus of being very fast!

Just 500 of Ford's super-fast Sierra Cosworth RS500s were built (by Tickford) so that the company could campaign the car in the European Touring Car Championship – the 2-litre, four-cylinder car gives a genuine 154mph, with astonishing acceleration as well.

S P E C I F I C A T I O N	
MODEL/TYPE	FORD SIERRA COSWORTH RS500
ENGINE	4-CYL, 1,994CC
HORSEPOWER	204BHP @ 6,000RPM
TRANSMISSION	5-SPEED MANUAL
CHASSIS	STEEL MONOCOQUE
BRAKES	4-WHEEL DISC
TOP SPEED	154MPH
ACCELERATION 0–60MPH	6.1 SECS
PRODUCTION SPAN	1987 ONLY

FORD

FORD SIERRA XR4

Striking though the Ford Sierra XR4 undoubtedly looked, the car never had the real performance to match, and as a consequence, it suffered the indignity of harsh road test criticism and relatively limited sales success. Ford was not to be caught out again by uniting wild styling with a gutless drivetrain – witness the outrageous and outrageously fast Sierra Cosworth.

The XR4 was withdrawn from the range in 1984 but there was a new model to supplant it — the Ford Sierra XR4×4. Not only does this version have a five-door body shell and a simpler lip spoiler on the boot in place of the XR4's twin-bladed 'tea trays', but it comes with full four-wheel drive and Ford's new 2.9-litre V6 engine.

The four-wheel drive system is made by FF in the UK and makes use of a centre epicyclic differential with viscous couplings in the rear differential and in the drive to the front wheels. Power is distributed slightly unevenly to front and rear wheels, those at the rear taking 64 per cent of torque to give a sporty feel to the car's handling and added grip on twisty country roads.

The gearbox which takes the drive from the new 2.9-litre engine has identical ratios for its five speeds. The engine itself is a vast improvement on the old, with low down torque far more readily available. This extra flexibility is not reflected in the unit's refinement, which is tappety at most speeds and harsh at very high revs. This car will still give 129mph and a decent 0–60 figure of 8.6 seconds although fuel consumption is unremarkable at 17mpg.

SPECIFICATION	
MODEL/TYPE	FORD SIERRA XR4×4
ENGINE	V6, 2,933CC
HORSEPOWER	150BHP @ 5,700RPM
TRANSMISSION	5-SPEED MANUAL
CHASSIS	STEEL MONOCOQUE
BRAKES	4-WHEEL DISC
TOP SPEED	129MPH
ACCELERATION 0–60MPH	8.6 SECS
PRODUCTION SPAN	1984→

With the four-wheel drive Sierra XR4×4, Ford has firmly dispelled the poor image that the last performance Sierra – the XR4i – was saddled with; not only are its looks less 'boy racer' but it also has more grip with its four driven wheels, and more go from a new 2.9-litre V6 engine.

F425 YCY

JAGUAR

JAGUAR SOVEREIGN 4-LITRE

Priced at launch at £32,500, the new Jaguar Sovereign 4-litre has to be something of a bargain. For not only is it a well-designed and carefully built executive saloon, it can also mix it with more overtly sporting competition. Despite its four doors and rather laid back styling, the Jaguar sporting pedigree is alive and well inside the new bored out 3980cc straight six.

Whisking its occupants to 60mph in 8.3 seconds, the Jaguar manages to cover the quarter mile in 16 seconds exactly. Mercedes and BMW are left well behind. But the real beauty of the 4 litre is the extra smoothness of the engine and improved ride and handling.

There have been other changes introduced to this top of the line model too. The semi-electronic instrument cluster found few friends among XJ6 owners and was dropped. Detail changes to trim and equipment show that Jaguar is listening to its customers, but it's behind the wheel that the 4-litre experience really tells.

Floor the throttle and the automatic gearbox will sprint through its four speeds on and on to around 140mph. Low-down torque has been increased, adding bite to the engine's response to a firm right foot prod. Switchable automatic 'boxes are becoming quite the rage among high performance executive machines, as they give drivers the choice of fully automatic or manual type driving conditions. Sport and economy modes also allow some discretion in change up speeds so a driver in a hurry can press on without the 'box changing up too low down the rev range.

Peak power comes in at 4,750rpm, but even under such strain the motor is barely audible. Fast cruising is a silent pleasure.

To provide efficient running and optimum control over the engine, Lucas have developed a fully digital ignition system for the 4-litre, the increase in capacity being the first major revision of the XJ6 series engines first introduced in 1983 in the XJ-S.

SPECIFICATION	
MODEL/TYPE	JAGUAR SOVEREIGN
ENGINE	6-cyl, 3,980CC, TWIN CAM
HORSEPOWER	235BHP @ 4,750RPM
TRANSMISSION	4-SP AUTO/5-SP MANUAL
CHASSIS	STEEL MONOCOQUE
BRAKES	4-WHEEL DISC
TOP SPEED	139MPH
ACCELERATION 0–100MPH	8.3 SECS
PRODUCTION SPAN	1989 →

The Daimler/Jaguar Sovereign 4-litre is possibly one of the finest high speed luxury executive cars in existence. While the occupants are cossetted in the finest of materials, the sweet AJ6 eats up the miles. The latest XJ6 is a smart looking car too, and despite the great visual resemblance to its earlier namesake, these cars have extremely well sorted chassis, up to the minute engine electronics, and a fair old turn of speed combined with excellent handling for such a large car.

G114 WHP

JAGUAR

JAGUAR XJS CONVERTIBLE

After dithering for over a decade, Coventry's foremost motor manufacturer finally got around to decapitating their lovely V12 super coupé, the XJ-S.

The result is a work of beauty, made even more pleasing due to the fact that sufficient care and attention went into the design of the hood to make it simple to erect and draught and flap-free. Electric operation saves fuss, and the blistering performance of the world's smoothest V12 produces an all-time great motoring package. Jaguar's engineers made up 108 new panels and modified almost 50 standard XJ-S panels for the new drophead, although the car closely resembles the tin-top coupé. This car drives like a hardtop even with the hood down; there's so little rattle, shake and flexing even when travelling rapidly along badly surfaced roads. The V12 coupled with a smooth operating

Jaguar's XJS, once the ugly duckling of the supercar set, is transformed into a svelte and stylish machine in convertible form; the car is remarkable solidly engineered and driving along country roads with the hood down is no problem – at the touch of a button the top can electrically erect itself should a dark cloud appear on the horizon.

three-speed auto box is the only powerplant available to the convertible, and there aren't many competitors who can match the Jag for grace and pace.

The ugly duckling which was the early XJ-S has indeed become a graceful swan.

S P E C I F I	C A T I O N
MODEL/TYPE	JAGUAR XJ-S CONVERTIBLE
ENGINE	V12, 5,345CC
HORSEPOWER	286BHP @ 5,150RPM
TRANSMISSION	3-SP AUTOMATIC
CHASSIS	STEEL MONOCOQUE
BRAKES	4-WHEEL DISC
TOP SPEED	144MPH
ACCELERATION 0–100MPH	8.0 SECS
PRODUCTION SPAN	1988 →

LOTUS

LOTUS EXCEL

As with Jaguar, I have selected two cars from the Lotus range, the Excel and the Esprit Turbo, to demonstrate the special Lotus qualities. In 1985 Lotus revised its specifications quite significantly, with new body styling, wheels and tyres, electrics, instruments, air conditioning, hard trim and soft trim.

The Excel has the performance to go with its good looks, with a top speed of 134mph and 0–100 in 20 seconds, with a fuel consumption of 29.4mpg at 75mph. A colleague who loves Porsches recently reported that he had tried a new Excel and was astonished not only at how well it performed but also at the very high standards of build quality. There is no denying that for far too long Lotus have had a very poor reputation for quality in their cars but in the last two or three years they have made great efforts to overcome these problems and it would appear that they are having success, which, happily, is being reflected in increasing sales.

The new certainly better looking than the old, it is cleaner and more 'of a piece' than before. The chassis is still the familiar steel backbone with a five-year anti-corrosion warranty. Thanks to the restyled body, the rear window is 25% bigger and access to the boot is much improved. New VDO instruments called Night Design have been relocated in the dash panel to better effect.

The engine is the 912-type 2.2-litre 16-valve double overhead cam four-cylinder unit, which produces 160bhp at 6,500 rpm. A five-speed gearbox is used and rear-wheel drive. All-independent suspension displays all the features that Lotus are famous for, the very highest levels of roadholding with no sacrifice to ride or comfort. Power-assistance to the rack-and-pinion steering is optional. Ventilated disc brakes are used all round and the system is servo-assisted. Alloy road wheels of 14 × 7in carry 205/60 VR 14 Goodyear NCT tyres.

SPECIFICATION	
MODEL/TYPE	LOTUS EXCEL
ENGINE	4-CYL, 2,174CC, SOHC
HORSEPOWER	160BHP @ 6,500RPM
TRANSMISSION	5-SPEED MANUAL
CHASSIS	STEEL BACKBONE
BRAKES	4-WHEEL DISC
TOP SPEED	134MPH
ACCELERATION 0–60MPH	7 SECS
PRODUCTION SPAN	1982 →

A subtle rounding out of the Lotus Excel's extremities has given looks to match the car's performance from the neat 16-valve four-cylinder engine *(opposite bottom)*. The four-seater Lotus is big but not heavy, quick but easily handled and exclusive but not unattainable.

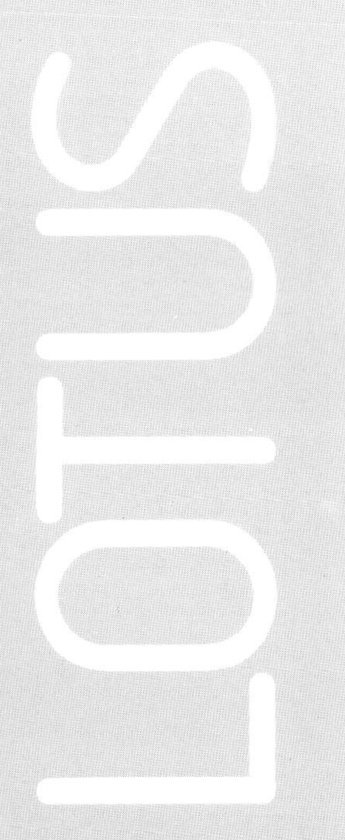

LOTUS ESPRIT TURBO

Lotus's Esprit shape dates back to 1974, when Giugiaro penned the mid-engined coupé as a styling exercise for the Norfolk company. The turbocharged engine option was announced in 1980, using the standard 2.2-litre Lotus four-cylinder engine with twin Dellorto carburettors and four valves per cylinder.

In 1988, however, the car was completely re-styled, retaining the basic concept of the car but endowing it with smooth, rounded bodywork that befits a fast two-seater sports car of the late eighties. This re-design was done in-house by Lotus stylist Peter Stevens. The car is not only better looking but it also has an improved aerodynamic profile and improved rigidity; on the minus side is a weight increase of 530lb.

The mid-engined Lotus Esprit Turbo amply demonstrates Lotus's late founder Colin Chapman's philosophy of 'no bloody compromise'. If you want this kind of performance you must travel light and if you don't want to hear the engine noise, buy a bike.

SPECIFICATION	
MODEL/TYPE	LOTUS ESPRIT TURBO
ENGINE	4-CYL, 2,174CC, SOHC
HORSEPOWER	215BHP @ 6,000RPM
TRANSMISSION	5-SPEED MANUAL
CHASSIS	STEEL BACKBONE
BRAKES	4-WHEEL DISC
TOP SPEED	152MPH
ACCELERATION 0–60MPH	5.4 SECS
PRODUCTION SPAN	1988 →

PANTHER

PANTHER SOLO

Although it's close to five years since the Panther Solo was first revealed as a motor show 'teaser', the first cars reached their expectant customers towards the end of 1989.

Those eager buyers must not be disappointed if Panther is to continue, for, despite a recent change in ownership (now by a Korean industrial combine), competition for the relatively small specialist car market is hot. The dramatically styled Solo was initially meant to be a cheap, British alternative to the phenomenally successful mid-engined Toyota MR2, but Panther wisely realized it could not hope to compete with the Japanese giant on manufacturing costs, so the Solo has gone up-market and up-tech. It uses the four-wheel drive drivetrain and turbocharged Cosworth 2-litre engine from the Ford Sierra Cosworth, the motor being placed in the chassis ahead of the rear wheels. The dramatic two-seater body is the work of Ken Greenley, the golden boy of London's Royal College of Art.

The British Panther Solo is not only a crucial car for its manufacturer, now under Korean ownership, but it's also vital to Britain's supercar credibility. Production, after a long gestation period, is now underway in a purpose-built factory and early press reports put great faith in the car's poise of handling.

SPECIFICATION	
MODEL/TYPE	**PANTHER SOLO**
ENGINE	**4-CYL, 1,993CC**
HORSEPOWER	**240BHP @ 6,000RPM**
TRANSMISSION	**5-SPEED 4WD**
CHASSIS	**STEEL SPACEFRAME WITH CENTRE TUB**
BRAKES	**4-WHEEL DISC**
TOP SPEED	**150MPH**
ACCELERATION 0–60MPH	**6 SECS**
PRODUCTION SPAN	**1989→**

TVR

SPECIFICATION	
MODEL/TYPE	**TVR 390SE**
ENGINE	**V8, 3,900CC**
HORSEPOWER	**275BHP @ 5,500RPM**
TRANSMISSION	**5-SPEED MANUAL**
CHASSIS	**STEEL BACKBONE**
BRAKES	**4-WHEEL DISC**
TOP SPEED	**150MPH**
ACCELERATION 0–60MPH	**5 SECS**
PRODUCTION SPAN	**1984 →**

TVR 390SE

Finally for this British section, I have chosen one model from the three car TVR range because it encompasses all that is excellent about this small, high quality car maker. The TVR 390SE is a front-engined, rear wheel-drive sports coupé using a separate steel chassis and a glass-reinforced plastic moulded body. Like those on the Lotus cars, this body is made in two halves, which are bonded along the waistline in the finishing process. The chassis is a multi-tubular steel backbone, very carefully protected against corrosion and with all-independent suspension. Braking is by ventilated disc units all round and rack and pinion steering is used. The 390SE rides on 225/50 VR 15 tyres, on alloy wheels. The 3,900cc V8 engine, derived from the Rover Vitesse unit, develops 275bhp at 5,500rpm and will whisk the TVR to over 150mph and from rest to 60mph in just 5 seconds, which puts it firmly in the supercar league. The engine uses Lucas electronic fuel injection and gives the car an average fuel consumption of between 20 and 25mpg.

In addition to the coupé, the 390SE can be ordered in convertible trim, although to my eyes the coupé is the better looking car. The TVR 390SE is a worthy competitor to several other fast cars and has the added advantage of being made by a company which takes great pride in its customer relations.

Hand-built by humans, not hand-built by robots, in a small factory in the seaside funfair town of Blackpool; the TVR 390iSE will out-accelerate virtually any production car in the world and offers a brand of exclusivity that more famous marques somehow lack.

JAPAN

Until recent years, the Japanese auto industry has concentrated mainly on producing transportation for millions of buyers world-wide who require no more than reliable, inexpensive cars. Their performance cars could be counted on the fingers of less than one hand but in the last four or five years that has begun to change and now there are several very worthy vehicles coming out of Japanese factories that, on their own merits, qualify for a place in this book.

A car that can probably make an honest claim to having been the first complete Japanese performance car must be the Datsun 240Z. The trouble with the 240Z is that the makers, Nissan, were so impressed by their success in the North American market that they fell into the trap of making regular changes to the car along the lines of giving it more comfort, more chromium plating, more styling features, more weight, more engine and more gadgets. All of that simply added more bulk to the whole car and gradually eroded the vehicle's initially impressive performance, making the last of the line, the 280ZX, into a caricature of the original (a pig's ear out of a near silk purse).

Japanese industry, however, whatever the product, has the flexibility and the long-range commercial vision to take heed of past mistakes and it also has the money to put them right, even if that means starting with a clean sheet of paper. There are now several Japanese cars that deserve close scrutiny.

The Japanese intend to leave no stone unturned in their attempt to dominate every segment of the market. New sports cars like the Mazda RX7 (above) and Honda NS-X (right) are the latest warnings to Europe to 'shape up or else . . .!'

NISSAN

NISSAN 300ZX

The 300ZX for the nineties is totally new in design, engineering and philosophy. For a start, it has dispensed with the fattened, showy, *boulevardier* looks of the outgoing car — it is so sleek and lithe that it could almost be a mid-engined machine, and Nissan give a drag figure of 0.31 which is a vast improvement on that of the old 300ZX. Powerhouse for this slinky little number is a development of the V6 used in the car's predecessor, but the cylinder head has been altered to incorporate a twin-cam, four valves-per-cylinder design. This, along with other modifications, contribute to an increase of power from 165bhp at 5200rpm to 222bhp at 4800rpm. Even more enthralling will be a twin Garrett turbocharged ZX which is reputed to give 300bhp at the rear wheels and whisk the lucky owner right the way up to 157mph. The standard, normally-aspirated car will be no slouch either — it, claims a glowing Nissan, will make it from zero to sixty in 7 seconds and give a top speed of 145mph. An additional feature for the turbo version, some might say a gimmic, will be Nissan's newly matured four-wheel steering system which steers the rear wheels briefly in the opposite direction to the front wheels

Although this will be the highest performing Nissan to date, the Japanese masters of competiveness will still kit the car's close-coupled interior out with all the gear, including six-way power-operated seats and a sophisticated Bose hi-fi system.

SPECIFICATION	
MODEL/TYPE	NISSAN 300ZX
ENGINE	V6, 2,960CC, DOHC
HORSEPOWER	222BHP @ 6,400RPM
TRANSMISSION	5-SPEED MANUAL
CHASSIS	STEEL MONOCOQUE
BRAKES	4-WHEEL DISC
TOP SPEED	145MPH
ACCELERATION 0–60MPH	7 SECS
PRODUCTION SPAN	1989→

NISSAN 200SX

Performance-wise, the 2005X is no slouch either, with 0–60 arriving in a blazing 7.2 seconds and a top speed of 140mph. The engine is turbocharged and intercooled and the standard equipment includes the obligatory anti-lock brakes (now deemed necessary on high performance cars) and a very good power-assisted system set-up. Yet, remarkably, the basic ingredients of this dashing Nissan are a 1.8-litre engine and rear-wheel drive.

Two new Nissan sports cars that show the former dullest of Japan's car makers is firmly on the ball are the brand new Nissan 200SX (right), and the stunning Nissan 300ZX (below), both designed for a discerning international market.

SPECIFICATION	
MODEL/TYPE	NISSAN 200SX
ENGINE	4-CYL, 1,809CC, DOHC TURBO
HORSEPOWER	171BHP @ 6,400RPM
TRANSMISSION	5-SPEED/3-SPEED AUTO
CHASSIS	STEEL MONOCOQUE
BRAKES	4-WHEEL DISC
TOP SPEED	140MPH
ACCELERATION 0–60MPH	7.2 SECS
PRODUCTION SPAN	1988 →

MITSUBISHI

MITSUBISHI STARION

When Mitsubishi showed its astonishing HSR ground-effect concept car a couple of years ago, it told the world that it wouldn't be long before the technology the car contained would make it into production.

There's nothing new in that, of course: every 'show' car revealed to the buying public is vaunted as 'the shape of things to come'.

But Mitsubishi has been more faithful to its word than most, because 1991's Starion replacement embodies much of the HSR's pacesetting equipment . . . especially in the area of what the maker calls 'active aerodynamics'. The HSR has given rise to the HSX 3000 GT – the car you see here – and this is itself a preview of what the 1991 car will be like.

The car's mechanical hardware is state-of-the-art high-tech: 3-litre, four-cam, V6 engine with twin intercooled turbo-chargers and 24 valves; drive, steering and anti-lock brakes to each wheel; computer-controlled independent suspension; five-speed Gatrag gearbox. It's in the stream-lining department that the HSX innovates. Aerodynamic principles are at odds with each other: you need minimum drag to enhance speed and fuel efficiency, but you also need downforce to make sure the car grips the road when it's being handled at high speed.

On the HSX both the front airdam and the rear spoiler are electronically extendable, using automatic sensors, so that the airflow around the car can be altered to suit the situation, ie: low drag on a straight, fast run, and higher drag during braking. These come into action at speeds of more than 50mph and although as yet unproven, the HSR concept car's six similar devices proved that the drag was adjustable from 0.20 to 0.40Cd, and that its coefficient of lift, od Cl could change from 0.00 on straights to 0.50 on corners. Gripping stuff indeed!

This sophistication won't come cheap but then the 1991 Starion will be vastly superior to the ageing and crude car it supplants.

The Mitsubishi HSX 3000GT (below) is a preview to the new Starion for 1991. It comes with all the high-tech equipment you would expect in a fast 1990s coupé, but with 'adjustable' aerodynamics to maximise its airflow and grip. Many drag lessons were learned from the HSR concept car (bottom left).

SPECIFICATION	
MODEL/TYPE	**MITSUBISHI HSX 3000GT**
ENGINE	**V6, 3,000CC, DOHC**
HORSEPOWER	**N/A**
TRANSMISSION	**5-SPEED MANUAL**
CHASSIS	**STEEL MONOCOQUE**
BRAKES	**4-WHEEL DISC**
TOP SPEED	**150MPH APPROX**
ACCELERATION 0–60MPH	**6 SECS APPROX**
PRODUCTION SPAN	**1991 →**

TOYOTA

TOYOTA SUPRA TURBO

Now, the Porsche 944 Turbo is a brilliant car for lovers of fast cars, but it's getting older and older — the basic body shape has been around since the 924 was introduced in 1975 and it's a familiar sight to most enthusiasts. So how about a car that can equal the performances of the Porsche 944 Turbo that's much newer . . . as well as costing half the price of the German car?

Toyota's recently announced turbocharged Supra offers just that — Porsche 944 Turbo 'go' for half the price, and an up-to-date shape.

Unfortunately, the hottest catalogue Toyota is not a car that oozes driver appeal, despite the fact that it will do 144mph and reaches 60mph from rest in a mere 6.9 seconds. It makes a good gadget-laden cross-country tourer but it lacks the verve of cars like the Toyota MR2 and four-wheel drive Celica, both acknowledged as frontrunners in the sports coupé sector.

The Toyota Supra — there is also a normally-aspirated version of the 3-litre twin-cam coupé for those who just want the basic car — still belongs to the seventies school of Japanese sports car thinking, a thesis that puts too much stress on luxury instead of ability. Therefore, as a well-equipped GT, the Supra scores. But not as a capable road sprinter!

SPECIFICATION	
MODEL/TYPE	TOYOTA SUPRA 3.0i TURBO
ENGINE	6-cyl, 2,954CC, DOHC TURBO
HORSEPOWER	232BHP @ 5,600RPM
TRANSMISSION	5-SPEED MANUAL
CHASSIS	STEEL MONOCOQUE
BRAKES	4-WHEEL DISC
TOP SPEED	144MPH
ACCELERATION 0–100MPH	6.9 SECS
PRODUCTION SPAN	1988 →

The Toyota Supra Turbo is a would-be Porsche 944 Turbo basher but its sheer driving poise is still not quite the match of the German car despite a luxuriously-trimmed interior and the customary load of Japanese gadgets.

F111 LPH

TOYOTA
F111 LPH

TOYOTA

TOYOTA MR2

The very latest in Toyota's fast car line-up is the long awaited MR2 sports coupé. This mid-engined device was announced to the British press in Portugal in January 1985, on a test route that was not in any way selected to pamper the cars but was capable of highlighting the smallest deficiency in their behaviour. After some time thrashing the MR2 around the mountains I was left with the impression, the firm impression, that with this car Toyota have a winner.

The car uses what must be the best mass-produced four-cylinder engine available in the world today, the twin-cam 4A-GE unit of 1,587cc capacity, which produces 122bhp at 6,600rpm and drives through a five-speed gearbox and transaxle arrangement. The MR2 will reach a top speed of 125mph and accelerate to 60mph from rest in 8.1 seconds. At a constant 75mph it has excellent 36.7mpg fuel economy. The electronic fuel-injection system gives instant starting, fast cold drive-away and superb response at all engine speeds, so good as to make the five-speed gearbox almost redundant!

I found just two small points of criticism to mention after driving the car. Firstly, the fuel tank is too small at only nine gallons, it really should be at least half as big again, and secondly the interior for someone of my (largish) size was just a little cramped. For two average-sized people wanting to cover long distances fast, however, with a reasonable luggage carrying capacity, the MR2 is superb. Steering, brakes, stability at speed, driving position, controls, finish, are all simply marvellous. In the vast quantities that Toyota are capable of making, the MR2 must be a distinct thorn in the side of many other fast coupé manufacturers the world over — and that is irrespective of any price considerations. It is certainly one of the best fast car bargains available today.

SPECIFICATION	
MODEL/TYPE	TOYOTA MR2
ENGINE	4-CYL, 1,587CC, DOHC
HORSEPOWER	122BHP @ 6,600RPM
TRANSMISSION	5-SPEED MANUAL
CHASSIS	STEEL MONOCOQUE
BRAKES	4-WHEEL DISC
TOP SPEED	125MPH
ACCELERATION 0–60MPH	8.1 SECS
PRODUCTION SPAN	1985 →

The pretty Toyota MR2 was the first small sports car to make serious inroads into what has traditionally been the territory of the British and Italian marques. Perhaps more importantly, it lifted Toyota's image as a provider of mundane saloon cars and estates and put it into a whole new category – that of the world of fast, capable cars.

MAZDA

MAZDA RX7

Although the latest shape Mazda RX7 looks very different from its predecessor, first introduced in 1978, the philosophy is just the same; that is, a top-class sports coupé that makes use of the NSU-pioneered Wankel rotary engine. Indeed, it is the only current production car to use this type of engine at the time of writing — although the latest Norton motorcyles also rely on rotary power. The Wankel engine has been around since the early sixties but it never caught on in road cars due to its fragility and high fuel consumption.

Mazda has stuck with it through thick and thin, and the engine is now as reliable as a normal piston combustion engine. It gives the RX7 a respectable top speed of 128mph and nought to sixty strutting ability in a mere 8.4 seconds, although poor fuel consumption is still something that Mazda RX7 owners and buyers will have to put up with — the car will not better about 18mpg.

When the car was tested by *Autocar* magazine in early 1988 the writer said that the car would benefit from the fitment — for the UK market — of a small turbocharger. This is now available to UK customers, and there is a new convertible version of the car on offer to lovers of fresh air motoring.

When introduced, the RX7 had its own, distinctively wedge-shaped bodystyle but Mazda consistently lost sales to its Porsche rivals in Stuttgart, so, as the Japanese firm is not allowed to use the Porsche name on its cars, it did the next best thing — it copied the 944's styling. Although the cars obviously differ in details, their overall shapes are very similar and it costs a competitive £16,499.

Mazda's RX7 Turbo has upheld the excellent reputation of its predecessor for a smooth, high performance coupé that is cheaper than its Porsche rivals: a penalty for using the Wankel rotary engine (right), however, is high fuel thirst.

SPECIFICATION	
MODEL/TYPE	MAZDA RX7
ENGINE	ROTARY, 2,300CC
HORSEPOWER	148BHP @ 6,500RPM
TRANSMISSION	5-SPEED MANUAL
CHASSIS	STEEL MONOCOQUE
BRAKES	4-WHEEL DISC
TOP SPEED	128MPH
ACCELERATION 0–60MPH	8.4 SECS
PRODUCTION SPAN	1986 →

HONDA

HONDA NS-X

The motor industries of Europe and America long ago recognized Japan as a world-class competitor in mass-production cars, but makers of fast cars never truly thought that the Japanese were capable of competing with them head-on, so there was much surprise when Honda revealed its NS-X sports car in February 1989, a sleek, mid-engined two-seater sports car aimed fairly and squarely at Ferrari and Porsche territory.

It is intended to be the flagship car of Honda's American Acura division and although shown initially in prototype form the car is expected to go into full production in Japan in 1990, at a projected rate of 5000 yearly — with three-fifths of that total going to America alone.

There's no doubt that NS-X — for New Sportscar X — looks sensational; the side scallops are a traditional Ferrari feature which always look good while the shark-nosed front end is pure Pininfarina 328GTB. At the rear, however, the car has an unusual, integrated spoiler and excellent all-round visibility through deep and generous windows.

No-one outside the factory had driven the car at the time of writing but its specification, an amalgam of high technology and traditional sports car engineering should ensure that the NS-X can reach Honda's claimed 155mph top speed and 0–62 acceleration time of a quick 6 seconds ... plus a standing quarter mile time of 'below 14 seconds". In the centre of the car, mounted transversely, is a brand new 3-litre V6 engine, with four-valves-per-cylinder. Complicated equipment like turbochargers and four-wheel drive are eschewed, but this 250bhp slingshot will have the security of anti-lock brakes and Honda's wheel-sensitive 'traction control' system. A five-speed gearbox will be standard. Italy and Germany had better watch out . . .

SPECIFICATION	
MODEL/TYPE	HONDA NS-X
ENGINE	V6, 3,000CC
HORSEPOWER	OVER 250BHP
TRANSMISSION	5-SPEED MANUAL
CHASSIS	STEEL MONOCOQUE
BRAKES	4-WHEEL DISC
TOP SPEED	155MPH
ACCELERATION 0–60MPH	UNDER 6 SECS
PRODUCTION SPAN	1989 →

Honda is pinning its supercar hopes on its new, mid-engined NS-X – for New Sportscar X – which is to be built in a brand new factory in Japan and is intended to be a flagship car for the firm's American Acura division; 250bhp and 155mph are promised . . .

HONDA

HONDA

USA

CHEVROLET CORVETTE

The standard Chevrolet Corvette is no longer the fastest American sports car, but there is no doubt that the Corvette is the longest running sporty car line still being made in the USA.

The Corvette was given a whole new set of clothes in 1982 but early examples of the car did not live up to the pre-production cars that had been shown to the press. Chevrolet took a great deal of criticism from expectant customers and frustrated road testers alike. So, in 1985, Chevy heavily revamped the car; the standard 5733cc V8, with fuel-injection, gives a rather measly 230bhp at 4000rpm, but torque is a useful 330lb ft at 3200rpm.

The beautiful two-seater body, also offered in convertible form, is one of the car's best features, while the interior, often fully leather-trimmed, features a great Delco/Bose sound system to compensate for the horrid digital instrumentation. 16mpg is possible.

But where the current Corvette is weak, the new Corvette ZR-1 — also referred to as the 'King Of The Hill' Corvette, will offer a truly stunning performance. Its V8 engine, and all-alloy 5.7-litre, has either 32 valves, giving a huge 380bhp at 6000rpm, or 16 valves giving about 200bhp, using an intriguing 'shut-down' mechanism that, at the touch of a dash-mounted key, closes eight of the inlet ports to limit the power and deadening half the engine's valves. The point of this is to safeguard novice drivers who might, somehow, find themselves behind the wheel of this fantastic motor car!

The engine, with its four camshafts and electronic fuel injection, was originally devised by Lotus, now part of the General Motors worldwide empire, and the British firm will make the 32-valve cylinder heds. The rest of the engine will be built up by Mercury Marine of Oklahoma, USA. A six-speed ZF manual gearbox handles the power of the car. No road tests had been carried out at the time of writing, but Chevrolet confidently expects 180mph-plus and 0–60 in just 5.6 seconds.

SPECIFICATION	
MODEL/TYPE	CHEVROLET CORVETTE ZR-1
ENGINE	V8, 5,727CC, DOHC
HORSEPOWER	380BHP @ 6,000RPM
TRANSMISSION	6-SPEED MANUAL
CHASSIS	STEEL FRAME/GRP BODY
BRAKES	4-WHEEL DISC
TOP SPEED	180MPH
ACCELERATION 0–60MPH	5.6 SECS
PRODUCTION SPAN	1989→

The All-American Sports Car is alive and well and living as the King of the Hill – the nickname for the fabulously fast Corvette ZR-1 (below) – just imagine being in this at the 180mph top speed that the car will do . . . or maybe the convertible version of the Corvette (left) is more your style . . .

FORD

FORD THUNDERBIRD

Ford's 1989 Thunderbird offering is yet another great all American sports car. Following on from the hugely popular 'aero look' from 1983, the 1989 model is the first all new shape since, and sets new styling standards. A ground up re-think of the '83 shape has produced a longer wheel base and wider track for the new T-bird, enhancing the handling and ride characteristics. The motive force for this American sports is a V6 3,800cc motor. Although the standard coupé boasts a respectable Cd of 0.31, the turbo coupé seems to falter a little with a Cd of 0.35.

Sequential electronic fuel injection, a standard five speed manual gearbox and turbo with intercooler allow this latest car to produce 215bhp @ 4,000rpm. The result is a quiet relaxed powerplant, peak torque (315 lft) being achieved at only 2,600 rpm.

All-round independent suspension with nitrogen gas shockers is adjusted automatically and all round power disc brakes with anti-lock are standard.

Inside the car, all dimensions have been increased to give added passenger space, though this risks the car becoming ungainly and overweight. Air conditioning, tinted glass and motorised safety belts are all included in the package. Power moonroof and CD player are 1989 Thunderbird options too.

There's no doubt that Ford are trying hard with this latest T-bird. The car certainly looks the part and with such a large amount of power at the driver's disposal, courtesy mainly of the turbocharger and intercooler, some spirited driving is to be expected. The relatively lazy engine, compared with some Italian sports machines, allows typically American style performance, though with the detailed changes in the suspension and chassis design for this latest car, ride and handling are surely an improvement on the old soft springing for which American cars were well known.

SPECIFICATION	
MODEL/TYPE	FORD THUNDERBIRD 1989 TURBO
ENGINE	V6, 3,800CC
HORSEPOWER	215BHP @ 4,000RPM
TRANSMISSION	5-SPEED MANUAL
CHASSIS	STEEL MONOCOQUE
BRAKES	4-WHEEL DISC
TOP SPEED	140MPH PLUS
ACCELERATION 0–60MPH	6 SECS
PRODUCTION SPAN	1988 →

The new Thunderbird design put on more weight for 1990. While enhancing passenger comfort by widening the interior dimensions of the cockpit, Ford have made the car seem larger than it really is. The T-bird now no longer resembles a lithe sporting coupe, but has fallen into the all too common trap of adding weight. Why can't the designers leave well alone? Having said that, the 1990 T-bird is still a fast comfortable cruiser, and in turbo form can see off much of the metal-cluttering American highways.

FORD

FORD MUSTANG GT

The Ford Mustang has always had a reputation as a fast car even if that reputation has not always been justified. Now, after some years in the doldrums, two new Mustangs have been offered to American buyers and these Mustangs really do have a claim as performance cars. The Mustang GT and the SVO models are significantly different in the way they go about being fast cars but in the end that is what they both prove to be. The GT model has a 5-litre pushrod V8 engine that develops a very unstressed 225bhp. It drives through a five-speed gearbox that seems just a touch heavy in operation, to a solid rear axle which is located by coil springs and 'Quadra-Shock' suspension.

The Mustang GT rides on handsome alloy wheels of 15-in diameter and which carry P225/60VR 15 Goodyear Eagle tyres. These fine tyres contribute a great deal to the Mustang's handling and stable ride. The whole car is very solidly built, the interior is well trimmed and only the masking of some of the instrument faces spoils the overall good impression.

Brakes are again a disappointing mixture of disc front and drum rear but in today's American driving environment they prove to be adequate rather than inspiring. Power-assisted rack-and-pinion steering is used, and I found this to be excellent.

From a performance point of view the GT is really good. It has bags of acceleration and Ford claim it will exceed 130mph, which I have no reason to doubt, having driven it. The GT version of the Mustang theme represents the ultimate expression of the traditional big American V8 in a small, or at least compact, body, this time with decent brakes and good roadholding as well. The Ford GT is also available in convertible form and, unusually for an American car, it cannot be ordered with an automatic gearbox!

SPECIFICATION	
MODEL/TYPE	FORD MUSTANG GT
ENGINE	V8, 5,000CC
HORSEPOWER	225BHP @ 4,200RPM
TRANSMISSION	5-SPEED MANUAL
CHASSIS	STEEL BACKBONE
BRAKES	DISC FRONT, DRUM REAR
TOP SPEED	125MPH
ACCELERATION 0–60MPH	N/A
PRODUCTION SPAN	1984→

127
D178 XVX

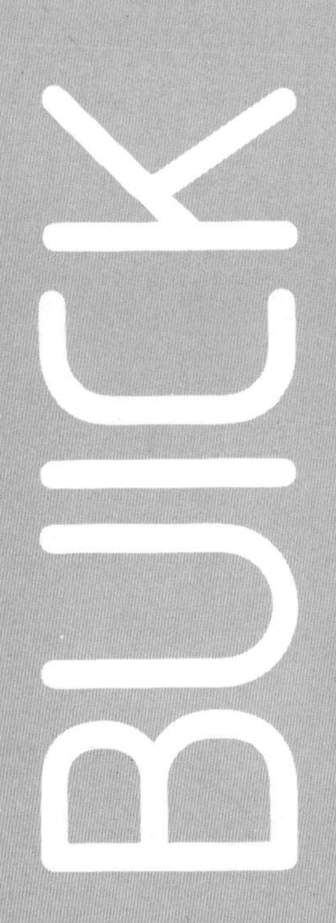

BUICK REATTA

Buick's revival as a sports car manufacturer has been aided immensely by the popularity of its latest offering, the Reatta Coupé. Launched only at the beginning of 1988, the Reatta has been so successful that Buick have taken the decision to introduce a full convertible version late in 1989.

However, some Reatta touches haven't found unanimous favour. Buick has removed most of the glitzy digital instruments from the dashboard and replaced them with good old analogue dials.

Under the bonnet lies a V6 3,800cc unit complete with balancer shaft for even smoother running. At 4,800rpm the engine is producing 165 bhp, aided by a complex sequential fuel injection system.

The body panels are made from galvanised steel and thermo plastic front bumpers prevent unsightly chips or dents.

The Reatta is no road burner in the conventional American sense, more a softened grand tourer. It comes complete with air conditioning, well appointed interior fittings, power windows and door locks and has a special electronic locking system.

Beneath the bodywork the chassis has been well sorted with anti-roll stabilisers sited at both ends. The direct acting stabiliser bars provide crisp handling and a good ride.

The smooth four speed automatic transmission takes the strain out of slipping cogs and there's a thoughtful overdrive provided for even better economy. The transmission fluid even has its own cooler, mounted forward of the radiator.

Steel-belted radial ply Eagle GT tyres hold the road with consummate ease, fitted to 15in alloy wheels. With all this go, stopping the Reatta is achieved via four discs protected from locking up by an advanced ABS system.

SPECIFICATION	
MODEL/TYPE	BUICK REATTA
ENGINE	V6, 3,800CC
HORSEPOWER	165BHP @ 4,800RPM
TRANSMISSION	4-SPEED AUTOMATIC
CHASSIS	STEEL MONOCOQUE
BRAKES	4-WHEEL DISC
TOP SPEED	120MPH
ACCELERATION 0–60MPH	8 SECS
PRODUCTION SPAN	1988 →

FORD

FORD MUSTANG SVO

Although it has very recently been dropped from production, the Ford Mustang SVO (Special Vehicles Operation) was the first step in the direction American Fords are taking. It represents the high-tech way of doing things — no more brute muscle as in the GT, but more of the subtler, European-type approach. That is, using turbochargers allied to relatively small engines, with digital electronic fuel injection and ignition systems to produce the horsepower. In the case of the SVO, a 2.3-litre, four-cylinder overhead cam engine and Garrett turbocharger produce 175bhp at 4400rpm. The EEC-IV computer-controlled blower allows an infinitely high 14psi.

The SVO's suspension has the excellent Koni dampers installed. Power-assisted rack and pinion steering is fitted and 16×7in cast alloy wheels carry P225/50VR 16 Goodyear tyres. This complete package gives the car very good handling and ride qualities. I have driven the car for considerable distances on freeways and minor roads of a very twisty nature and at all speeds the SVO stuck to the road as though it was glued there! The handling in corners, fast and slow, was excellent, supplemented by the fine steering. The brakes, unlike those on the GT, are ventilated discs at the front and rear, and power-assisted, of course.

A 200% Porsche fan I have known for some years surprised me with his enthusiasm for the SVO. He liked the car so much that he sold his current Porsche and ordered one of these very special Fords. He called it the best all-round value car in America, and was eager to take delivery.

The SVO, however, is now recent history, replaced by Ford's new 'personal' sports coupé, the Mazda-built Probe. Whether it will have the same appeal and dynamic allure is uncertain. The Mustang has been allowed a stay of execution, however, in 2.3-litre LX and 5-litre GT versions, and long may it remain.

SPECIFICATION	
MODEL/TYPE	FORD MUSTANG SVO
ENGINE	4-CYL, 2,300CC, TURBO
HORSEPOWER	175BHP @ 4,400RPM
TRANSMISSION	5-SPEED MANUAL
CHASSIS	STEEL MONOCOQUE
BRAKES	4-WHEEL DISC
TOP SPEED	OVER 125MPH
ACCELERATION 0–60MPH	7.76 SECS
PRODUCTION SPAN	1984–1988

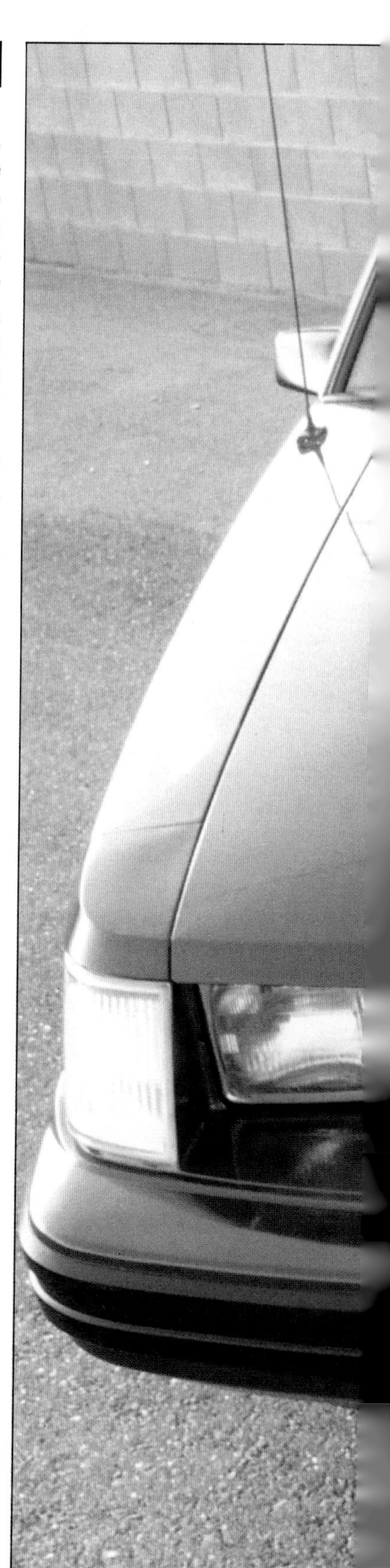

The cockpit *(above)* of the Ford Mustang SVO *(left)* shows America's growing acceptance of the more restrained interior styling of European cars—especially sporting models.

CITROEN XM

The French have been making fast cars for as long as anyone else, but for some time now they haven't had more than one or two really quick, specialist-built cars suich as the Facel Vega or the shortlived Monica. But now they make some excellent fast machines, ranging from the pint-sized Renault 5 Turbo through to the 16-valve version of the Peugeot 405 and the blistering turbocharged Renault 21 Turbo saloon. There's even a French rival to the Lotus Esprit, the Renault 25 V6-powered MVS Venturi, said to be capable of over 140mph. Some of the swiftest of recent French cars have been so-called 'homologation' specials, like the formidable Peugoet 205 Turbo 16 described overleaf, highly specialized machines devised principally for rally domination in the heady days when Group B regulations allowed rally cars to develop into fire-breathing horsepower oozers. A series of horrific accidents killed the breed, and France's new power image is in the hands of cars like the new Citroën XM.

Citroën's brand new top-range executive car, the XM, has the difficult task of upholding the traditions laid down first by the DS and then the CX — the turbo-charged GTi version of which was cpapble of a thunderous 136mph. The top XM, so-named to recapture some of the drama and sparkle of the glorious Maserati-engined SM coupé of the early seventies, comes with a 3-litre, fuel-injected V6 in place of the GTi's ancient four-cylinder powerpack, giving 170bhp. Combined with a drag factor for the dramatic Bertone-styled bodywork of a mere 0.28, the top XM — the 3-litre V6 Injection — will give over 140mph. And just in case you're worried that Citroën's individuality is slipping away, the XM comes with a revolutionary 'Hydractive' computer-controlled pneumatic suspension system which alters the car's stance whenever its speed changes.

Citroen's dramatic new XM, 1989's Car of the Year champion, has set new standards for ride comfort and handling – it has also placated Citroën fans who were alarmed at the fact that recent Citroën products have been losing their idiosyncratic and unusual character.

SPECIFICATION	
MODEL/TYPE	CITROËN XM
ENGINE	V6, 2,975CC
HORSEPOWER	170BHP @ 5,600RPM
TRANSMISSION	5-SPEED MANUAL
CHASSIS	STEEL MONOCOQUE
BRAKES	4-WHEEL DISC
TOP SPEED	140MPH
ACCELERATION 0–60MPH	7.5 SECS
PRODUCTION SPAN	1989 →

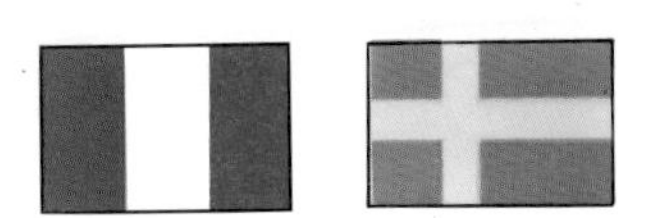

XM

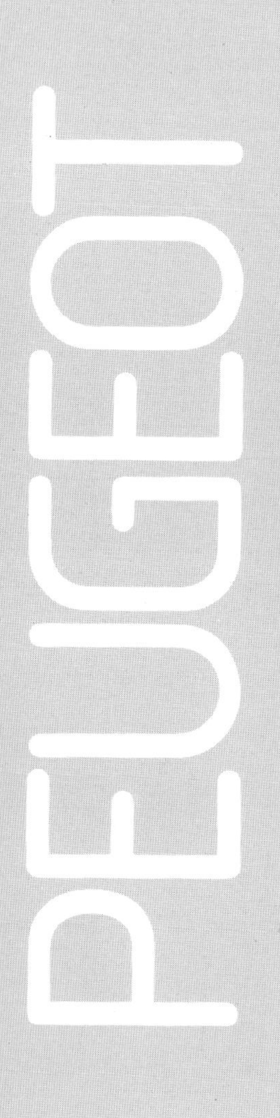

SPECIFICATION	
MODEL/TYPE	PEUGEOT 205 TURBO 16
ENGINE	4-CYL, 1,775CC, TURBO
HORSEPOWER	200BHP @ 7,250RPM
TRANSMISSION	5-SPEED MANUAL
CHASSIS	MONOCOQUE/TUBULAR
BRAKES	4-WHEEL DISC
TOP SPEED	130MPH PLUS
ACCELERATION 0–60MPH	5.8 SECS
PRODUCTION SPAN	1984 →

PEUGEOT 205 TURBO 16

When the Peugeot 205 model range was announced, early in 1983, it created a sensation. The 205 had up-to-date styling, fine performance, very good ride and handling and it had what no other Peugeot had had before, it had chic — a charm that drew the customers into Peugeot dealerships in their thousands. The company has had to increase production rates of the car several times over in the two years since then to meet the demand. With their super GTi model the demand shot up again with the 205, Peugeot could do no wrong.

The company also went rallying, but with a car that was even more outstanding: the 205 turbocharged 16-valve-engined, four-wheel-drive machine. They won rallies, including the 1985 Monte Carlo, in which they took first, third and fifth places overall. To be able to enter this extraordinary car in international competition Peugeot had to build at least 200 customer examples, which they have done, and they have sold every available car.

On seeing the car for the first time it is obvious even to the uninitiated that this is a racer. It could be nothing else, with its big wheels, the air intake for the mid-mounted engine, the spoilers — they all go to state that this is not a normal drive-to-the-station commuter car. The 1,775cc engine uses four valves per cylinder and is blown by an intercooled German-made KKK turbocharger. It churns out 200bhp at 7,250rpm and there is little real power under 3,000rpm but once the tachometer needle hits 4,000rpm things really start to happen. If it were not for the four-wheel-drive arrangement the car would be difficult to control.

Driving this competition-inspired vehicle calls for firm and positive action on the part of the driver, the Peugeot has to be made to obey directions and this is no car to pussyfoot around, it has to be dominated. There is little, if any, luggage room in the car, it is noisy and can be tiring to drive far, but the *fun* factor is sky-high.

The Peugeot 205 Turbo 16 in works competition guise ended the Audi Quattro's near monopoly of rally wins in 1984 and the model is also now available as a rather special road car.

SAAB

SAAB 9000T

Apart from their rally cars, Saab have never had a reputation for building wild, fast, ultra-exciting vehicles. Sensible — yes; functional — yes; very well made — yes; but *not* cars that get the blood boiling, more cars of the head than of the heart. With Saab's new 900 16S and 9000 models however, there could well be a change in the wind.

The 9000's styling has none of that 'Look at Me, I'm a Super Car' gimmickry that others go for. It is a sober, functional shape, with enormous interior space, a well laid out set of instruments and controls to aid the driver at his task and, under the bonnet, all the latest sophistication to be expected of a fourth generation turbo-car.

It undoubtedly goes; a factory claim of over 135mph has been confirmed in many road-tests. It has stability at speed, it has excellent roadholding and ride qualities, it shows all the effort put into it after ten years of painstaking research and development. The 1,985cc four-cylinder engine has four valves per cylinder and double overhead cams. The inter-cooled turbo unit produces a full 175bhp but there is a problem, or rather two problems with the 9000. Its steering is lacking in feel, which doesn't help the strong understeering nature of the chassis, and there is a disconcerting 'On-Off' character in the engine's power delivery. Both of these items can make it difficult to drive the 9000 fast in the dry and very difficult in the wet. Power delivery goes from almost nothing to full blast in a spread of only 500rpm.

Maybe the answer to the steering response lies in the tyre size, because they do appear to be on the narrow side. By the time it is in the dealers' showrooms these small deficiencies will undoubtedly be sorted out.

SPECIFICATION	
MODEL/TYPE	SAAB 9000T
ENGINE	4-CYL, 1,985CC, DOHC
HORSEPOWER	175BHP @ 5,500RPM
TRANSMISSION	5-SPEED MANUAL
CHASSIS	STEEL MONOCOQUE
BRAKES	4-WHEEL DISC
TOP SPEED	130MPH
ACCELERATION 0–60MPH	8.2 SECS
PRODUCTION SPAN	1985

The Saab 9000 (top) continues the Swedish company's recent tradition of fast, sporty, executive saloons while the 900 convertible (main picture) sees Saab entering the new world of 'niche' markets where specialised cars like dropheads are attracting new customers.

F797 NJH
turbo
F741NJH

Index